BRIEF
INSIGHTS
ON MASTERING
BIBLE STUDY

Also by Michael S. Heiser

Brief Insights on Mastering the Bible
Brief Insights on Mastering Bible Doctrine

BRIEF
INSIGHTS
ON MASTERING
BIBLE STUDY

80 Expert Insights,
Explained in a Single Minute

60-SECOND SCHOLAR SERIES

MICHAEL S. HEISER

ZONDERVAN®

ZONDERVAN

Brief Insights on Mastering Bible Study
Copyright © 2018 by Michael S. Heiser

This title is also available as a Zondervan ebook.

Requests for information should be addressed to:
Zondervan, *3900 Sparks Dr. SE, Grand Rapids, Michigan 49546*

Library of Congress Cataloging-in-Publication Data

Names: Heiser, Michael S., author.
Title: Brief insights on mastering Bible study : 80 expert insights, explained in
    a single minute / Michael S. Heiser.
Description: Grand Rapids, MI : Zondervan, [2018] | Series: 60-second
    scholar series | Includes bibliographical references.
Identifiers: LCCN 2017054258 | ISBN 9780310566564 (softcover)
Subjects: LCSH: Bible--Study and teaching.
Classification: LCC BS600.3 .H443 2018 | DDC 220.071--dc23 LC record
    available at https://lccn.loc.gov/2017054258

Cover design: Rick Szuecs Design
Cover art: www.flaticon.com
Interior design: Kait Lamphere

To Dave and Wayne Burggraff, my first pastors,
who ignited my interest in Bible study

CONTENTS

Part 2. Understand What the Bible— and What Your Particular Bible—Is

Part 3. Accurately Interpret the Bible

Part 4. Bible Study Tools

INTRODUCTION

Another book on Bible study? Well, yes and no. For sure, my aim in this book is to help readers progress in their ability to study the Bible and understand its meaning. But this isn't like other books on Bible study. I'm not concerned with teaching you a method. Instead, I'm interested in being honest about what will help you and what won't.

Let's start with a cold dose of truth. As a Bible scholar with more than twenty years of teaching experience, I can tell you that effective Bible study doesn't happen by making the books of the Bible conform to a method. You can learn to repeat steps and follow rote procedures, but that won't produce greater comprehension of what Scripture teaches its readers.

The reason is simple. Biblical writers didn't write with a study method in mind. Books of the Bible can be quite different, so they don't conform to canned approaches. If you've tried one of those Bible study methods books, you know I'm telling you the truth. Sure, you learn to write notes, draw in your Bible, and fill blanks in books. But learning tasks isn't grasping what the biblical writers wanted you to see and understand.

There are certainly techniques you can use to study Scripture more adeptly. I'll give you a few of those in this book. But a technique that helps you in one instance may not help you in another. You need a tool chest, not a checklist. How you approach the Bible needs to be flexible and adjustable, not rigid and repeatable.

The key to good Bible study isn't following steps. It's learning to think carefully about what you're reading. You develop thinking skills by asking insightful questions, learning to detect and avoid flawed ideas (your own and those of others), and being dissatisfied with explanations that aren't comprehensive. Learning to think well is much more powerful than memorizing a method. Careful thinking allows you to adapt to whatever Scripture presents you rather than asking the same questions of every passage.

Much of what you'll read in *Brief Insights on Mastering Bible Study* is therefore aimed at giving readers sound advice. It's filled with dos, don'ts, and blunt advice I might suggest if I was peeking over your shoulder as you study. I've used all of my own recommendations. Some are more obvious than others. Yet they'll all help you move to the next level in getting more from your Bible study.

PART 1
STUDY HABITS

CHAPTER 1

Read the Bible with a Critical Eye—It Can Take It

Christians revere the Bible. That's understandable. After all, it's God's Word, the authoritative source for truths we affirm, errors we deny, and the sort of character we strive to develop. Consequently, its sacred status might cause us to flinch at the suggestion that we should question what it says and scrutinize its contents. It feels a little like we're judging a book that ought to be judging us.

Is our hesitation biblical? And, dare I ask, is it rational? Frankly, the answer is "no" in both cases.

The Bible has been fulfilling the roles described above for millennia despite repeated and relentless attempts to destroy it, undermine it, ridicule it, and marginalize it. But it's still here. In fact, today there are more Bibles in circulation in more languages than at any time in world history. How could we possibly harm it by asking it to make sense and then pursuing that goal?

The response that subjecting the Bible to critical analysis hurts *us* is equally incoherent, primarily because the Bible itself encourages its own scrutiny. Ezra is esteemed for his commitment to study (Ezra 7:10). Luke regards the close examination of the Scriptures as a virtue (Acts 17:11). Biblical writers not only quote Scripture but take care to observe minute details like the specific form of words (Gal. 3:16).

We are God's imager-bearers. God is the most rational being there can be. We share in his attribute. We are not commanded, nor does the Bible ever suggest, that we read Scripture *irrationally* or without the intellectual abilities for rational thought that God shares with us. Have you ever tried to read *anything* irrationally? It sort of defeats the purpose of written communication.

Critical thinking is akin to any other human ability—speech, strength, creativity, resourcefulness—and it's ours to employ in loyal service to the true God. Approaching Scripture with a passive, anesthetized mind will not protect Scripture from criticism. It needs no protection. Intellectual laziness in search of truth is no virtue.

CHAPTER 2

Thinking Is Better than Memorizing

When I was a freshman in Bible college, one of my professors was something of a zealot for Bible memorization. During the semester he had us memorize 150 verses, punctuation included, using the King James Version. I had an excellent short-term memory, so the feat wasn't that hard. I've since read the Bible in several versions, but I still recall a lot of Scripture in the KJV. In that respect, I'm still living off the capital of that investment in memorization.

While I'm thankful for the discipline of that class, I feel compelled to state something obvious: memorization isn't Bible study. Memorization is, well, committing something to memory for later recall. But being able to recollect a verse with precision does not mean you understand it. You could memorize your tax forms, but that isn't going to resolve any confusion that may arise from what they say. It's the same with Scripture. I could memorize the entire Bible, but how does that nurture my comprehension? My precise recall would be the same as simply reading the text word-for-word had I never bothered to memorize it. Whether reciting or reading, I might not know what any of it means in any given place.

My point is not to call for a memorization boycott. Nor is it an opportunity for revenge on my college professor. Rather, my aim is for you to realize that memorization and study are not interchangeable concepts. Real Bible study demands *thinking*. Memorizing words is not the same as pondering what words mean.

For example, you could easily commit the following sentence to memory: "New Study of Obesity Looks for Larger Test Group." Knowing what the words mean, though, takes some reflection . . . and a sense of humor.

Many things we read, especially in the Bible, aren't as easy to parse as this headline. Many readers will have memorized Ephesians 2:8–9:

> For by grace you have been saved through faith. And this is not your own doing; it is the gift of God, not a result of works, so that no one may boast.

But how many of us have bothered to ask the obvious question: *What* is the gift of God? Is it grace? Faith? Both? Something else? How would we know? Memorizing these verses is a good idea, but understanding what they mean is even better.

CHAPTER 3

Bible Reading Is Not Bible Study

You should read your Bible. That's axiomatic for Christians, and I'd dispense that piece of advice to anyone. But reading the Bible is not where our engagement with the Bible ends. It's where it begins. You need to go beyond reading the Bible to serious study of the Bible. The first step is to realize there's a significant difference between reading and studying.

Reading is casual, something done for pleasure. The motivation is personal gratification or enrichment, not mastery of the content. Bible reading has as its aim private delight or personal application for our lives and relationship with God. Bible *reading* is inherently devotional and low maintenance.

Bible *study*, on the other hand, involves concentration and exertion. We have an intuitive sense that study requires some sort of method or technique and probably certain types of tools or aids. When we study the Bible, we're asking questions, thinking about context, forming judgments, and looking for more information.

It's not hard to illustrate the difference. Almost anyone can make a cup of coffee, but they're not baristas. We know instinctively that both perform the same basic task, but what distinguishes the barista is a lot of time, effort, research, and experience in learned technique. It's the same with Bible study.

Let's try another coffee illustration. Let's say you and your friend were from the moon and didn't know what coffee was. You're only mildly interested in the topic, so you decide to look it up in a dictionary. You read that coffee is "a popular beverage made from the roasted and pulverized seeds of a coffee plant." Good enough. You learned something. But your friend wants to know more—a lot more. How is coffee made? What's the process? Is there more than one process? If so, why would there be different processes? Is there more than one kind of coffee bean? Where are the beans grown? Does that make any difference in color, aroma, or flavor? Is climate a consideration? How is coffee different than tea? If it's a popular beverage, how much is consumed? Does consumption vary by country? State? Gender? Age?

Whoa. She's way over the top. And we know why. Her intensity of interest and willingness to expend effort tell us her aim is studying, not just reading. There's a big difference, and it's one that translates well to what we should do with the Bible.

CHAPTER 4

Bible Study Is a Discipline, Not a Ritual Event

Two of the hardest things about serious Bible study are getting started and then sustaining the effort. While a word like "sustaining" naturally speaks of regularity and continuity, I'm not talking about treating Bible study like your morning routine. I'm not suggesting you make it part of a routine at all. If routine helps, then have a go at it. Being faithful at something doesn't mean always doing it the same way or at the same time. All too often spending time studying Scripture deteriorates into an item on a checklist to be dutifully checked off. "I'm devoted now."

Since Bible study is more than Bible reading, by definition it involves thinking. Thinking is work. It's not for sissies. If you're not mentally tired after doing what you presume is thinking, you aren't really thinking. Sometimes our days don't afford the time for the kind of sustained effort that goes into serious Bible study. Don't let that bother you. Rather than fret over missing the study session your put on your checklist, my advice is to devote the small increments of time that you have to just thinking about what you've studied before. Sometimes it's better to evaluate what you've taken in rather than taking in more.

The point is this: It's more spiritually productive to develop clarity on a point of the text or to figure out a way to frame a question for future study, than to just mark time with an open book (even if it's the Bible) for the sake of maintaining a daily ritual. Ultimately, Bible study is about developing aptitude in the Scriptures, the source material for knowing God, not scorekeeping.

The life of the mind can be cultivated anywhere. You always bring your mind with you. Whatever you've been studying lately can be brought back and worked over again. Your brain has stored the fruits of your study. Precise recall isn't a prerequisite either. Retrieve some thought and probe it for weakness, or thank God for its clarity. You'll be surprised at how simply thinking from time to time helps you process a given issue or problem in altogether fresh ways.

CHAPTER 5

Insist on Being a Slave to the Text—Let It Be Your Master

I've been in academia for almost thirty years, both as a graduate student and a professor. I've spent time in both Christian and secular institutions. My Christian experience taught me the fundamentally important lesson of having a high view of Scripture. Treat it as God's Word. My secular years taught me a lesson just as valuable, and one that I didn't find consistently in a Christian context: be a slave to the text.

In my secular experience, being a slave to the text meant that you shouldn't bring prior commitments to the biblical text you're studying. Theological ideas about how the text came about or how it might be understood to achieve a theological outcome should be left behind. The text is all that matters. Theological commitments are irrelevant and, in fact, impediments to understanding.

This is, of course, what one would expect in a secular institution. They aren't seminaries. However, there's a bit of a flaw in this understanding. Objectivity is a myth. No one can jettison all preconceptions about something, no matter what the context. The secular scholar has presupposition of his or her own that crouch in the mind, ready to influence interpretation. I knew that, so I took that part with a grain of salt. But the lesson wasn't lost. The text is all that matters, so we must let the text take us wherever it leads.

Ironically, despite the pervading belief in inspiration, I didn't see this principle consistently practiced in Christian academia. True, any given seminary has, and needs to have, certain theological commitments, but those theological commitments should not be the basis of judging scholarship or handing out grades. Rather, professors should be forthright. They should have well-informed exegetical arguments for their positions (presumably those of the school) but should be honest with the text. They should admit that, given other interpretations about the Hebrew or Greek grammar and word usage here and there, the conclusions drawn from a passage could be different. To hide those possibilities or manipulate the text to your "obvious" conclusions is dishonest.

So it should be with personal Bible study. The *text* is what is inspired, and nothing else. Loyalty to God's Word means letting it be your master. By definition, your interpretation or belief *cannot* be biblical if it does not derive from the text.

CHAPTER 6

The Goal of Bible Study Shouldn't Be a Spiritual Buzz

Every earnest believer wants their study of Scripture to make a difference in their lives and the lives of others. I'm not suggesting it should be expected or will always happen, but productive and meaningful Bible study should move you emotionally from time to time.

I realize that last sentence is contrary to what many of you have been taught or perhaps read. What do I mean "from time to time"? Shouldn't we always be emotionally touched by Bible study? My answer is that if you're doing Bible study to *feel* a particular way, or get some spiritual high, your Bible study is self-focused. To be blunt, that's the antithesis of Bible study.

Bible study is not about you. It's about gaining knowledge of God and his plan through the means he gave you for that end: the Bible. This doesn't mean that we don't learn about God in any other way. Yet God prompted people to write long ago so that those of us living today would know certain things about him, his plan for humanity, Jesus Christ, and how to be in right relationship to him through Jesus. Nowhere are we taught in the Bible to "search the Scriptures to feel a certain way."

The perspective of Bible study against which I'm arguing has, to my mind, reduced the role of the Spirit to tingling our emotions.

As a result of that outlook, weak-minded believers are tossed about by the elasticity of their feelings and circumstances, and fall easy prey to clever articulations of bad theology—even within the church.

Real Bible study ought to produce careful thinkers about truth. As we expose ourselves to Scripture and submit to what it teaches us on its own terms, the Spirit will illumine our minds and use that understanding to move us emotionally, whether that be to a profound sense of peace, satisfaction, guilt, or repentance. Too often we read or study Scripture with an unconscious demand: "Lord, I'm reading this now, give me that feeling I really need to get through my day." Bible study is not a narcotic. You can't have a true sense of knowing God—and the emotional impact that brings—without the discipline of being in the Word of God. God knows what you need. He will honor your loyalty.

CHAPTER 7

Deuteronomy 29:29 Is No Excuse for Intellectual Laziness in Bible Study

No one likes to hear excuses. Whether it be your kids, your parents, your coworkers, or your friends, it's downright annoying when people try to avoid problems and then make excuses for not doing what they know needs to be done. It's something we all have to police in ourselves too—and in our Bible study.

Deuteronomy 29:29 has unfortunately become the go-to verse for quitting when thinking gets hard in Bible study. It's the verse that says:

> The secret things belong to the LORD our God, but the things that are revealed belong to us and to our children forever, that we may do all the words of this law.

Most people only know the first few words: "the secret things belong to the LORD." As a professor and a Bible teacher in church, I've heard those words often enough to be able to paraphrase their meaning whenever they're used by students of all varieties and circumstances:

- "No one really knows what that verse means, so can we move on to something more practical?"

- "I want my Bible to be simple. You're making my head hurt."
- "Are you going to ask us to explain that passage on an exam?"

The irony here is that Deuteronomy 29:29 doesn't mean that there are things in the Bible that are hard to figure out. Deuteronomy 29 is part of the conclusion of a long sermon by Moses about blessings or curses from God for obedience or disobedience. After talking about the need to obey God and how to avoid offending him, Moses punctuates his point with this verse. The point is not that God says things that are difficult to understand. It's that concealed acts of sin are still known to God. They will be punished by him since they are known by him. The revealed violations were the Israelites' responsibility to punish.

For our purposes, the point should be clear: Deuteronomy 29:29 is not about waving the white flag of surrender in Bible study. No one understands everything in the Bible, but a lot of hard passages really do have coherent explanations. It's our job to find them, not evade the work involved.

CHAPTER 8

When You Read about a Place in the Bible, Look up What Happened There

I've never liked geography. It was one of the more boring classes I had in high school. The only value I ever saw in it was learning about maps. But even that became sort of useless once I learned that AAA would create trip guides for you that highlighted the route you needed to take. Now the internet does that too. And when you visit other countries, you get a tour guide. Who needs to pay attention to places and locations, especially in a book as old as the Bible?

You do.

Surprisingly enough, I didn't have to be dragged kicking and screaming to that conclusion. Reading an article about the biblical region of Bashan changed my attitude. After finishing that essay, I could not see the word "Bashan" in Scripture without thinking about it the way ancient Israelites thought about it. That's when the lights went on.

Because they have histories, places have reputations. What do you think of when you read the words "Las Vegas"? How about "Ground Zero," "Normandy," "Boston Harbor," and "Washington, DC"? Each one comes with its own set of images drawn from important and ongoing events. We can't see these place names without all sorts of ideas and memories flooding our minds.

The same is true with biblical places. But most ancient place names don't resonate with us since we know so little of their history. Biblical writers dropped place names all the time. When they noted in passing that a biblical character went to a location or did something at a particular place, their readers knew instantly what the geography telegraphed.

For example, it's significant that Joshua gathered all the tribes of Israel at Shechem to renew the covenant with God (Josh. 24:1). Shechem had a history, both good and bad. In the horrible stories of Judges 19–21, there are reasons why the author keeps dropping geographical hints about the characters. The place names drive the stories because of the associations they conjured in the mind of the reader. Paul's urgent passion to get to Spain (Rom. 15:24, 28) has a compelling Old Testament backdrop.

Curious about these examples? Good. You have work to do! Discovering what a location is known for will help you think thoughts the author wanted you to have.

CHAPTER 9

Read Journal Articles

When people see the word "journal" they think of a diary or travelogue. Those aren't what I'm talking about. I'm thinking of academic research journals. Granted, academic journals make for challenging reading. They are written by scholars for scholars and their students (pastors, seminarians, or graduate students). But there's nothing like them for biblical research. Since they are published a few times every year, they are more up-to-date than commentaries and Bible dictionaries. They are the cutting edge.

Academic journals are like magazines. They usually have between five and ten articles covering a hundred or so pages. But they are *not* magazines. There are crucial differences.

Journal content is peer-reviewed. Articles that appear in a magazine like TIME are not submitted to a panel of field experts. They are written by journalists who may or may not have academic exposure to the field of their article. For example, there is a clear difference in tone and quality between an article on Alzheimer's that appears in the Journal of the American Medical Society (JAMA) and TIME magazine. An article in TIME will be written for nonspecialists and have a strictly imposed word count. It's a diluted summary of the topic. You get the basics. However, an article in the former may run thirty pages, use technical vocabulary, and will have undergone peer review. It's scientific research discussed by experts. You get all the hard data.

You ought to know about scholarly journals in biblical studies and read them from time to time. Major news magazines seem to annually produce hit pieces on the historicity of Jesus and the Gospels every Christmas and Easter. What readers get in those articles is the work of a journalist, not a scholar. That journalist might interview a handful of scholars for a half-dozen quotations. Those are sound bites. You're getting crumbs that a nonexpert with no expert supervision decides you need to read.

As a serious Bible student, you should know that anything you'd ever read in a popular magazine about the Bible is selective in content and guided by an editorial agenda. Academic journals will show you what experts in the field, of all theological persuasions, including those with a high view of the Bible, are actually saying. Read them.

CHAPTER 10

Look up Cross-References

Any seasoned Bible reader knows what cross-references are: chapter and verse references inserted in your Bible near (or within) the verses you're actually reading. Print Bibles use several conventions for cross-references. A typical strategy places tiny superscripted numbers or letters next to words that correspond to other verse references located somewhere else on the page, usually the bottom. A key principle in Bible study is letting the Bible interpret itself. Cross-references are an important gateway to letting that happen.

The purpose of cross-references is to alert you to other verses in the Bible that say something similar. For example, let's say we're in Ephesians 1, and we come to verse 7: "In him we have redemption through his blood, the forgiveness of our trespasses, according to the riches of his grace." My copy of the ESV puts superscripted letters next to several words in that verse: in, redemption, through, forgiveness, according. Those letters give me a total of ten cross-references to other verses that reiterate or develop the ideas of Ephesians 1:7.

The more cross-references you can find, the better. Many concepts in Scripture are threaded throughout its pages, not just echoed here and there. When Scripture becomes a commentary on Scripture for you, you're starting to do biblical theology.

Ten cross-references may sound like a lot, but it isn't. My ESV

Study Bible lists nearly ten more verses that I could look up in regard to Ephesians 1:7. But you can do a lot better than that.

One of the tools every Bible student should have, in print or digital form, is *The Treasury of Scripture Knowledge*. The latest edition (the "New Treasury"; 1992) claims to be "the most complete listing of cross references available anywhere." It's not an idle boast. The entire book is a compilation of cross-references. That's right—a book full of nothing but lists of verses. No prose. It's *wonderful*. It provides nearly forty cross-references for Ephesians 1:7.

The Treasury of Scripture Knowledge is most conveniently used within a Bible software platform. The speed saves you a lot of time. But even in hard copy, this is a must-have tool.

CHAPTER 11

Bible Study Isn't like Marriage

Every reader who is married knows that marriage is an adjustment. The honeymoon phase does indeed end. Couples may love each other, but conflict eventually surfaces. One piece of sage advice for handling conflicts that I received sometime after getting married was offered in the form of a question: Do you want to be *happy*, or do you want to be *right*? I caught the drift. Winning a debate and making your spouse happy aren't interchangeable ideas.

While this advice works well for marital bliss, it doesn't work for Bible study. When it comes to interpreting Scripture, you want to be right. Flawed analysis and poorly formed conclusions about what the Bible says aren't going to produce Bible study bliss. In the long run of our spiritual lives, getting warm and fuzzy feelings from a misunderstood passage is far less desirable than grasping the text accurately without a wave of emotion sweeping over us.

The same can be said about having your own theological comfort zone as your goal for Bible study. If we believe the text is inspired, we need to be subservient to what it says, even when our efforts produce results that conflict with what we've been taught to believe. If we're teaching others, our goal cannot be keeping people happy with what we discover are flawed beliefs and interpretations. Bible study is meaningless if we aren't striving to understand God's Word correctly.

So remember that you aren't practicing marital diplomacy when you study Scripture. Think critically. Be tenacious. Demand clarity. Giving in isn't going to make God happy. He wants you to wrestle with his Word and get it right.

CHAPTER 12

"Study" Is a Verb

B efore I decided to go to graduate school, I spent some time in seminary. One of my professors was known for memorable phrases. One of his off-the-cuff quips has stuck with me for decades: "If you don't think the ministry is hard work, you aren't in it." I never went into the pastorate, but that phrase rings through the corridors of my mind whenever I think about Bible study. It lends itself to a suitable adaptation: If you don't think Bible study is work, you aren't doing it.

Bible study is *work*. The word "study" implies activity and effort. I know from experience that this truism is foreign to many. There are reasons for that.

Some people never graduate from Bible reading to Bible study. Reading doesn't require much effort, especially if you aren't thinking while doing it. Running your eyes over words on a page is one of the easiest things an adult does at any given point of their day. But Bible reading isn't Bible study.

Others associate Bible study with "getting a blessing." This confuses devotional reading with study. The goal of Bible study isn't a spiritual buzz. Bible study isn't in search of a feeling. It's in search of understanding what the biblical text says and what it means. That isn't to suggest personal application is irrelevant or ought to be avoided. Instead, it's to suggest that "applying" anything in the Bible without knowing what it means is at best useless and at worst dangerous.

41

Another reason is that small group Bible studies are usually passive. Little actual study happens, at least for anyone other than the person tasked with leading the group. While the leader may have put serious work into the effort, everyone else is a listener. True, the material may stimulate questions, but asking a question isn't Bible study. It's where Bible study often begins.

Most of us know that "study" is a verb. You know that if you went to college, prepared for your driver's license exam, wanted to research a pending medical procedure, or are serious about fantasy sports. A better synonym for Bible study than "reading" would be "research." And research isn't easy. It takes tools, tenacity, and time.

CHAPTER 13

The Aim of Bible Study Is the Meaning of the Text, Not a Defense of Your View

The Bible is God's Word—a repository of truths and information that, through human authors, God wanted preserved for posterity. Since the Bible is one of God's means to transform our lives and direct our behavior, those who hold it in esteem have an emotional investment in it. They believe that it's the expression of God's will, not only for faith but also practice (2 Tim. 3:16–17).

Given all that's riding on Bible study, it's not hard to see why people who engage in it seriously sometimes argue about the results. Disagreements aren't about an intellectual victory. Right and wrong are at stake; at least that's the ideal. Sometimes that's accurate. Other times it's exaggerated.

Knowing exactly what the Bible means at every turn would require omniscience. There are a number of passages that are ambiguous. God knows omniscience isn't an attribute we possess. Consequently, assigning a point of morality to every interpretive decision is unwise. It may sound sacrilegious, but a lot of the Bible—and hence, Bible study—doesn't have a moral issue in view.

I've met many Christians who are so desperate to make sure their behavior is right and not wrong that they end up becoming better at arguing for what their family or tradition tells them a verse means than actually studying the matter for themselves. I've seen relationships destroyed over conflicting Bible interpretations where no core doctrinal teaching was at stake. I've seen believers driven to despair when friends or family members make an interpretation a litmus test for good standing before them, and even before God.

The goal of Bible study shouldn't be about finding ammunition to make someone guilty, or shaming someone on the other side of a disagreement. It isn't about finding ways to crush opposition or force a spiritual submission. You aren't the Holy Spirit. It's often better to kindly share what you believe and its basis in Scripture and then privately take your concerns to the Lord.

CHAPTER 14

Ignorance Is Not a Gift of the Spirit

In this era of social media, we've all been exposed to people who have a knack for irritating and offending people they've never met. If you peruse comments on blogs or online forums to any extent, you know precisely who I'm talking about: the person who just can't seem to read anything without making sure everyone learns that they disagree and why, often in copious detail. So much for the global community.

I've been blogging for years. I've seen countless samples of incoherent, apoplectic screed. Those don't bother me. The dialogue I find disturbing hits me in my soft ministry underbelly. As someone who's spent many years in the classroom as a biblical studies professor, I care that people want to learn Scripture. In my experience, a single overbearing spirit can poison the learning environment with disturbing speed and efficiency. The internet is the natural habitat of the indociles textus habitantis (Latin for "unteachable web dweller").

You would think it would be easy for a professor to (pardon the pun) teach this type of student a lesson. But this species often comes with an immunity: their appeal to ignorance as a virtue. Bringing up why the unteachable soul needs to rethink their dogmatic conclusion because of a point of Greek or Hebrew grammar has little effect when they've been trained to be suspicious of scholars. Appeals to Christian charity are harmlessly deflected when the target equates being uninfluenced by research with "defending the faith" (a tortured use of Jude 3).

I'm not recommending that Bible students bow to everything scholars say. For one thing, that would be impossible since scholars often disagree. For another, even scholarly conclusions are influenced by presuppositions. A committed Bible student needs to respect scholarship, not genuflect to it.

No one earns a PhD without learning a great deal. That effort does indeed separate the scholar from most people. But the way to judge what a scholar says is not by extoling the virtues of ignorance. Instead, the committed Bible student will put in long hours to either confirm or critique what a given scholar says.

God doesn't smile with more affection on someone who knows little about a subject, especially when that subject is the Bible. Willful resistance to thinking hard and long about the book we say is inspired is anything but a gift of the Spirit.

CHAPTER 15

Use a Variety of Methods in Bible Study

Variety is the spice of life, so the saying goes. It's good advice for Bible study. The principle is obvious. While there's security in routine, it's nice to mix things up once in a while or try something new. Change invites our problem-solving intelligence to kick in and, consequently, to stimulate our brain.

There are a lot of approaches to Bible study. You might want to try as many as you can discover, or master just a few.

Since most people graduate to Bible study from Bible reading, the verse-by-verse method is often where people start. The method involves moving through a paragraph or passage looking up cross-references, picking words to study, and figuring out what every sentence means within the larger unit.

Topical Bible study is an entirely different method. Topical Bible study is just what it sounds like—discovering what the Bible says about a given topic. This method would require tools that can get you started in sketching out a topic, like Bible dictionaries. You need to know up front what the key words are that relate to a given topic. For example, if you wanted to study Old Testament sacrifices, you wouldn't just use a concordance to look up the word "sacrifice." You'd also want to look up words like "offering," "blood," "sprinkle," and "atone." Once you have a range of key words, you'll discover the key passages.

Another method is doing character sketches, also known as biographical Bible study. This approach focuses on a single Bible character, searching for every passage where he or she appears. In this method you need to be on the alert for where the character's name doesn't appear, too. Sometimes a character is just named by a pronoun ("he" or "she" did this or that). The goal is to build a profile of what that person was like. How did your character react in given circumstances? What can the episodes of his or her life tell you about their personal strengths and weaknesses? How did they relate to God? Sometimes unnamed characters can be the focus of this kind of study. A Bible study on women in the Gospels, named or unnamed, could be quite interesting.

Even this handful of methods can keep you engaged for a long time. Be on the lookout for others and try something new!

CHAPTER 16

Questions Are Not Answers

There's nothing better for keeping you humble as a Bible teacher than a critique by your spouse. Mine once told me that I had the irritating habit of leaving questions unanswered when I taught Scripture. I'll admit that I like to do that. My explanation was that people need to know that there's a lot to think about in the Bible—that they don't have it down like they think they do. I also told her that I wanted them to keep coming back for more.

She wasn't fazed.

I think my reasons made sense, but I also have to admit that her criticism was valid and important too. People don't like to be left in an intellectual and spiritual lurch when it comes to the Bible. Scholars thrive on open questions. It's like releasing a squirrel in front of a dog. But most of us want closure on whatever is being talked about. Those of us who spend a lot of time in Bible study need to remember that, since we're often the ones who will be teaching others.

It's a hard lesson to learn. Serious Bible students like pursuing questions too. There's a certain "thrill of the hunt" feeling that comes with detecting a problem, framing it, and then attacking it. There's also a compulsion to be honest. Sometimes conclusions really aren't available or aren't clear in our minds. But think of how frustrating it would be if, in the process of doing research, the sources you depended on were ambivalent, never quite coming to a conclusion.

This advice is pertinent to Bible study itself. We should seek conclusions when we study Scripture, especially when a passage is crucial to some point of doctrine. Granted, the Bible is clearer in some places than others, but if your Bible study results in everything being open-ended, there's a problem with either your method or analysis, and perhaps both.

The moral of this story is that you need to land the plane in Bible study, even though you know it'll take off again. It's okay to reach tentative conclusions and allow yourself to revisit an issue later. But at least come down somewhere, for your sanity and the sanity of others.

CHAPTER 17

The Guidance of the Spirit Is Neither a Remedy nor an Excuse for Lackluster Bible Study

If you've watched a baseball or football game on television at some point this century, there's no doubt you've seen players either ask God for success or thank him for it. Athletes today regularly do things like point to the heavens after crossing home plate or finding themselves in the end zone. Some will bow in a short prayer. It's a nice sentiment and, for many, a testimony that transcends a token gesture.

But let's be honest. Unless that football player gets in shape and memorizes the playbook, all the pointing to heaven in the world isn't going to lead to success. You can say a short prayer on the mound or in the batter's box, but unless you can hit the strike zone or a curveball, you're going to fail. Pretty badly, in fact.

It's the same in Bible study. All too often people who sincerely want the feeling of knowing Scripture aren't willing to put in the time it takes to get there. Instead, they'll take short cuts and then expect the Spirit to take up the slack. The assumption seems to be that the promise of the Spirit to guide us into truth means the third person of the Trinity will excuse a lack of effort and give us the answers we need. The analogy that comes to my mind when I hear that is a little disturbing. The Spirit isn't the kid sitting next to you in high school that lets you cheat off their exam. *Do your own work.*

Setting aside for the moment the fact that passages like John 16:13 really aren't about personal Bible study, the truth is that God expects effort in the pursuit of truth. The Spirit of God works in our hearts and minds, which are the terms Scripture uses for our intellectual faculties (i.e., our brains). He generally makes use of the content you've put there (in your brain) in your pursuit of the truths of Scripture. There's no mental download from heaven coming.

Rather than substitute the Spirit for personal effort, my advice is this: as you do the hard work of Bible study, ask the Spirit for insight to expose flawed thinking (your own or whoever you're reading) and for good questions to ask about the biblical text. The more of God's Word you've devoted attention to, the more the Spirit can help you recall for understanding.

CHAPTER 18

Attention to Detail and Clear Thinking Are Not Antithetical to Loving Jesus

Sometimes people mistake inquisitiveness for criticism. Early in my own spiritual journey, I was consumed with knowing Scripture. I'd ask questions, listen to answers, and then follow up with more questions. Sometimes it irritated people. I can recall several instances in church or home Bible studies where I was scolded about obsessing over the Bible. After all, I was told, the real point of Bible study was learning about Jesus and how to follow him.

I disagreed then and still do. Wanting to know why women who had their periods were considered unclean, what the Urim and Thummim were, or why some English translations of John 5 don't include verse 4 isn't about wanting to know more about Jesus. But they're good questions. Frankly, there are a lot of passages in the Bible that have nothing to do with Jesus. The fact that they're in the Bible means they're just as inspired as any passage that *is* about Jesus. We either believe all of Scripture is God's Word and "profitable for teaching, for reproof, for correction, and for training in righteousness" (2 Tim. 3:16), or we don't.

You don't need to repent if you're not content with someone's explanation of a passage. It's not a spiritual flaw to want details and precise answers, especially in regard to something as important

53

as the Bible. Saying the goal of Bible study is about being a better disciple misrepresents both Bible study and discipleship. They're related but not synonyms. Dampening someone's thirst for knowing Scripture by making them feel less spiritual isn't part of discipleship. In my experience, it's more a sign of personal insecurity. We should be thrilled when we encounter someone who just can't get enough of the Bible.

Bible study is about learning what this book that we say is inspired actually means. Knowing what all its parts mean will give us a deeper appreciation for the plan of God for humanity, the salvation history of God's people, and the character of God. Jesus is at the core of all that, but there's more to the Bible than the story of his life, death, and resurrection. If that was all God wanted us to know, he'd have given us only the four Gospels. It's evident he had more in mind.

CHAPTER 19

Bible Study Is about Discovering the Meaning of the Text, Not Deciding How to Apply the Text

I spent two summers during college as a pastoral intern. I enjoyed it, though the experience contributed to the realization that I wasn't cut out for pastoral ministry. I knew my calling was different. Something I did during that time also taught me a lot about what Bible study wasn't—or at least shouldn't be.

One of the periodic tasks of pastoral interns was, unsurprisingly, preaching. We were allowed to pick pretty much any passage for a sermon and were given a generous amount of time to prepare. I had a couple years of Bible college coursework under my belt, so I wasn't new to Bible study. The only instruction that was given to me was that preaching wasn't teaching.

I understood the intent of the instruction: don't turn the sermon into a classroom session. That's good advice for several reasons. But it made the task incredibly difficult. I finally concluded that all I needed to do was go through the passage, make an observation here and there, and apply those observations to people's spiritual lives—to our aspirations, failures, God's forgiveness, and the need for consistency as followers of Jesus.

The formula worked wonderfully. I got a lot of positive affirmation from the pastoral staff and people in the pew. A couple days later, though, I had an epiphany that soured the experience but was just what I needed. I realized that I had preached a well-structured outline, not the text. Instead of really grappling with the meaning of the text, conveying that to people, and then drawing out lessons rooted in the text, I'd used the Bible to make people feel a certain way. *They'd been challenged spiritually but hadn't learned a thing about the passage.* I had manipulated my audience when my job was to help them learn Scripture and respond to it in their walk with God.

Bible study shouldn't be an exercise in being clever. When we look into Scripture only to jog our minds about what we're doing right or wrong, or how someone else is pleasing God or not, we aren't doing Bible study. Bible study should be about understanding what Scripture says and teaches. The Spirit will take the fruit of that labor and challenge hearts. We're no substitute.

CHAPTER 20

Don't Allow Anyone to Protect You from the Bible

I did my doctoral work at the University of Wisconsin-Madison and had four years of teaching experience by the time I left. One of the things I tried to instill in my students was they shouldn't allow anyone to shelter them from difficult or controversial passages in Scripture, even from obvious conclusions that didn't seem to jibe with their traditions. The Bible should be approached with openness. We must be willing for it to dictate the terms of what we believe rather than filter it through denominational distinctions or ideas we prefer.

I had this lesson reinforced after moving and looking for a church to attend. We happened upon one that started to feel like a fit. The pastor had a degree from a well-known seminary and was a good speaker. His first two sermons from 1 Peter on our first two visits were solid expositions. The people were friendly and there were kids the same age as our own. It was even close to our apartment. Then week number three happened. It wasn't pretty.

Our third visit coincided with the pastor preaching on 1 Peter 3:14–22, a very odd passage that is one of my favorites. What happened next is something I'll never forget. The pastor took the pulpit and said with complete sincerity that he was skipping the passage. He transparently explained that it was too strange to understand and, so far as he could tell, had no important role for theology.

The incident sticks with me for several reasons. The complete, unabashed surrender to ignorance was troubling enough. More troubling was the mixed message his decision telegraphed. The church was in a tradition that was heavily invested in a handful of modern creeds. His decision either implied that passages that were "consistent" with creedal formulations somehow had more to offer or that the people in the pew needed protection from their own Bible lest they somehow be doctrinally "confused" by material the creeds hadn't made digestible for them.

When we do Bible study, we are often helped by the words of men and women who have devoted themselves to biblical scholarship. But the true object of Bible study is the biblical text. We do not need to be protected from Scripture. We need to be dedicated to understanding it—*all of it*.

CHAPTER 21

Believe That God Will Help You

G od wants us to understand Scripture. It stands to reason, then, that he's perfectly willing to help us do that. I'm not talking about including a formulaic prayer for assistance when you begin your Bible study. I'm not recommending a specific prayer at all, though that's appropriate. I'm suggesting that you go into Bible study *expecting* God to help you with something he already wants you to do.

I learned this lesson in some startling ways in graduate school. I chose a controversial topic for my dissertation. Granted, every dissertation is supposed to blaze a new path, but mine had an element of risk. I was bucking consensus opinions because I thought I'd noticed something unaddressed in centuries (really, millennia) of scholarship about the Hebrew Bible. In grad school, it isn't enough to say, "I don't think the way everyone else does." You have to offer something coherent and defend it well enough to please a room full of top-tier scholars.

One day I walked into the library absorbed with a particularly vexing problem that I couldn't unravel in my mind. I was there because I'd come across a reference to an essay in a book that sounded like it might be useful. I went to the stacks to get the volume and, inexplicably, it wasn't there. The computer catalogue said it had not been checked out, but all I saw on the shelf was a rectangular hole. I had to get to work, so I turned around to leave.

My eye fell on a random book whose title I'd never seen. Something told me to open it. I did. To my astonishment there was an essay in the Table of Contents on precisely what I was struggling with.

I hadn't prayed before that first incident, but I knew God was looking out for me. I'd do my research and go to the library and just tell God I needed direction. I was being honest. There were times I felt lost with my topic.

God helped me. The experience I described above was repeated a half-dozen times while writing my dissertation. It got to the point where I wouldn't leave the library without checking the books on either side of one I'd come for. I always checked the shelf behind me, too!

CHAPTER 22

Believing What the Bible Says Isn't Bible Study

Not all of the obstacles to studying the Bible are negative (*not* having enough time, *not* being sure you'll do it right, *not* feeling smart enough, *not* knowing where to start, etc.). Sometimes it's what we affirm that gets in the way.

I've been a Christian for over thirty years. I've been to a lot of churches, talked to a lot of people, and taught a pile of Sunday school sessions. I've taught thousands of students in Bible classes over the years. I'm sympathetic to people whose fears impede their progress in Bible study. I've been there, so none of those uncertainties irritate me. But one excuse I've heard over the years really pushes my buttons: *I already believe what's in the Bible, so why do I need to study it?* Just typing it makes me growl.

Think about what such a statement really says:

- What I know and believe is the important stuff.
- My faith is based on something someone told me.
- I believe what I can't necessarily explain and might not really understand.

It may sound harsh, but the presumption that our faith exempts us from thinking clearly about what we believe reveals both a lack of faith and personal insecurity. We fear our beliefs cannot stand scrutiny or that we don't have the mental muscle to probe Scripture deeply. Frankly, we've been conditioned to embrace such flawed conclusions by our own communities. Churches are filled with people who are sincere about their faith. They aren't waffling about the basics of the faith. And if basically every sermon goes back to the simple gospel message, it's reasonable for them to conclude it makes little sense to study what they already embrace.

That may have "worked" decades ago, but we're living in a different world now. Parents and pastors are no longer the gate-keepers of information and truth. Google and YouTube are. The next generation, and a good bit of your generation, aren't listening to only Christian voices.

I'm not suggesting that evangelism or the health of the church in the next generation depends on being able to win debates (though losing them will certainly not help). It's true that people turn from the Bible despite having access to sound thinking. Immaturity, worldliness, and rebellion are all factors. What I'm saying is if you cannot give a coherent "reason for the hope that is in you" (1 Peter 3:15) that goes beyond what your parents or your pastor told you, your voice will be no more credible than anyone else whose beliefs are just hand-me-downs.

CHAPTER 23

Five Minutes Is a Long Time

Growing up, no one taught me the Bible. My first exposure to the Bible that I can remember happened when I was about ten years old. My best friend's mom had a devotional time with her kids. If I was there, I was invited to stay. I was amazed that kids my age and younger knew the names of Bible characters and stories. About all I knew was Adam, Eve, and Jesus (at least the names).

There were times I'd sit in that little Bible study feeling like the dumbest person in the room. I guess I was when it came to the Bible. I wanted to know more, but it felt like an impossible task. Today, I'm a Bible scholar with advanced degrees who studies Scripture in the original languages. I'm light years from where I started.

Trust me, it didn't happen overnight. What I know now is the cumulative result of thousands of incremental sessions of studying Scripture and hundreds of resources related to it. It had to be that way, since I worked full time through fifteen years of graduate school, and most of my time in college before that.

One of the most helpful things I've ever heard was something a professor told us during freshman orientation at college. One of our orientation sessions was about time management. The professor looked out over the auditorium and then changed my life when she said *five minutes is a long time*. If you've ever had to wait five minutes for something (a favorite show, an appointment, the bathroom!) you know it's true.

I took her advice to heart. If I had five minutes to read or review something, I took it. It's amazing how much data can pile up in your brain in small bits. I got through college and graduate school and did well. I still can't stand to be idle. I'm always trying to learn about something.

I understand what it means to be pressed for time. Making time for Bible study is a legitimate challenge, especially if you're an adult with a job, kids, and a string of responsibilities. If you only have five minutes for careful Bible study, take it. It will add up. I'm living proof that it works.

CHAPTER 24

Listening to a Sermon
Isn't Bible Study

One of the constants in church life is complaining about sermons. Pity the pastor! It isn't an easy task to capture people's attention with the Bible. To many people in church, it's a totally foreign book that they don't believe they can understand. Others think they've heard everything already, so their minds are prone to wander.

Since you're reading this book, it's a sure bet the above doesn't describe you. You want to learn Scripture and don't think you've absorbed all that there is to see in Scripture. You come to church expecting to learn something. That's all very good. I just don't want to see you fall into the trap (or pattern) of substituting the Sunday sermon for Bible study.

If you're the kind of person that takes notes during a sermon, you may wonder about where I'm going here. I'm talking about the person who *doesn't* take notes—who is a completely passive listener. I've known many people that, when asked if they study the Bible, think that's what they're doing when they talk about the sermon in a small group. That isn't Bible study. It's sharing opinions about what someone else thinks about a Bible passage. Bible study isn't an opinion survey.

If you take notes during a sermon, you've already moved beyond the passive act of listening. Taking notes during sermons can convert sermon time into Bible study time. I actually recommend it, though I've known plenty of people that almost say it's a sin because "sermons are spiritual exhortations, not lectures." A pious false dichotomy is still a false dichotomy. Shutting off your brain in church isn't a virtue.

Taking notes during sermons prepares you for Bible study. If you happen to be working through the same passage in your Bible study, you can look up cross-references while you listen or jot down questions the sermon raises in your mind. Even if you aren't in that passage, if you take careful notes, you'll be able to pick up your thoughts in the future when you study that passage. You're way ahead of the curve if your notes are digital; those things are searchable!

So go ahead—make the sermon a time to sharpen some Bible study skills. God won't mind.

CHAPTER 25

It's Never Too Late to Start Studying the Bible

I've met people over the years who want to get serious about Bible study but think it's too late. Some are new to the faith and "past their prime" as they'd put it. Others have been Christians for decades but have never taken the time to get into Scripture in a way that moves beyond occasionally reading the Bible. Most of the time when people say those things, I know they aren't making up an excuse. They really do believe it's too late.

If that's you, take this in the right spirit: that's *nonsense.*

Studying the Bible is as easy as moving beyond reading in simple ways: looking up cross-references, using the concordance in the back of your Bible, reading through notes in a study Bible, thinking critically about what you see and probing it with questions.

Experts like to say it takes 10,000 hours to become an expert in something. That's nonsense too, unless you want to be a sports Hall of Famer, perform surgery, practice law, or be a lead chef at a five-star restaurant. I'm not talking about getting a PhD in biblical studies. That isn't a requirement for being a serious Bible student. I'm talking about becoming proficient at using certain techniques and tools and then being tenacious in their use. Five minutes a day every day will achieve that. I know because I've done it.

Proficiency in Bible study is about perseverance, not intellect or intuition. Most of the things we'd consider ourselves good at are like that. Sure, you can read about a kid who has a photographic memory who became a chess grandmaster before he was ten, but 99.9 percent of chess experts aren't that kid. They got to their proficiency through repetition.

Age is no obstacle to this either. An eighty-year-old who devotes time every day to Bible study will have a year's worth of experience (and knowledge) by their next birthday, exactly the same as if a thirty-year-old did it. What matters is actually *doing* it. The mind has an amazing ability to store information and recognize patterns. It just has to be trained through repetition.

So don't put off getting into Scripture. Everyone you know will be a year older at this time next year, but only those who actually engage in Bible study will know Scripture any better.

CHAPTER 26

Follow Someone Who Leaves a Trail

A good strategy for becoming adept at Bible study is to find a mentor, someone who models skilled Bible study and can pass on what they know. That transmission happens either by verbal instruction or modeling. In a perfect world, one's pastor would fill this space. I was blessed to have a pastor who took us through the text. I didn't know it, but I was learning to study the Bible. If you can say the same, thank God for your pastor.

However, I've heard hundreds of complaints from Christians about the lack of biblical content from the pulpit in their church. Granted, I may be hearing a distorted number of those laments because I interact with people online. But other lines of evidence have convinced me there may be a deep problem in this regard.

First, some recent studies have confirmed the vacuous state of biblical knowledge in Christian churches, including those in the evangelical orbit. A 2009 Barna Group study sent shockwaves through thousands of churches after it reported significant declines in biblical literacy and engagement of the Bible among churchgoers between the ages of eighteen and forty-four. This was offset by a rise among the same group in desire for "Bible knowledge." The divergence suggests a disconnect between what people want and what they're often getting in church.

Second, I have regular exposure to the books being produced by pastors and lay teachers for the church at large. Many of them are light on biblical and theological content, focusing instead on advice, encouragement, and cultural engagement. Those things are good, but they don't feed the hunger for biblical content.

Pastors have a difficult job. Most are insanely busy with administration, counseling, visitation, and meetings. They have little time to study Scripture in depth. But that recognition doesn't solve the problem. Christians are starving for serious biblical content, not the basics of the faith with adult illustrations. If pastors don't preach and text the text, they don't provide a template for how to study Scripture. If you can't retrace your pastor's sermon in the biblical text after Sunday, you may need to find a mentor somewhere else.

PART 2

UNDERSTAND WHAT THE BIBLE— AND WHAT YOUR PARTICULAR BIBLE—IS

CHAPTER 27

The Old Testament Came before the New Testament

I know what you're thinking. *How profound. Talk about having a firm grasp on the obvious.* Fair enough. But some of the most important keys for Bible study are hidden in plain sight. This thought is utterly crucial, and one most Bible students miss despite its transparency. To be honest, there are few things more important for biblical theology than having this fact invade your mind and establish a permanent beachhead.

Even someone who's never read the Bible can discover that the Old Testament came before the New Testament. That's what the Table of Contents is for. Yet even seasoned Christians read and study the Bible as if that observation is more a point of trivia than an indispensable clue to competent Bible study. I know of preachers who don't consider the Old Testament worthy of pulpit time. I've had many sincere Christians tell me they can't recall the last time their pastor went through an Old Testament book. The average person in the pew has been conditioned to equate the word "Bible" with "Jesus" or "the Gospels" or "the book of Revelation." Don't believe me? Ask fifty people in your church this question, and see what answers you get: "What's the Bible about?" Most answers will sound like you asked what the New Testament was about.

Ignorance of the Old Testament is a serious issue. I'd call it a hermeneutical crime. Since it came before the New Testament, it was the Bible of Jesus, the apostles, and the first Christians. The Old Testament is *three-quarters* of your Bible today. The New Testament books quote from it for a simple reason: New Testament theology is tethered to Old Testament theology. Since it came first, it has "coherence priority"—it is *essential* for understanding what follows. There isn't a page of the New Testament that doesn't reference the Old Testament in some way. Every New Testament doctrine has its roots in the Old Testament.

We like to say that Scripture must be interpreted in context. *The Old Testament is the primary context for the New Testament.* Without a grasp of the purpose and theology of the Old Testament, any commitment to context forfeits its authenticity.

CHAPTER 28

Read the Preface to Your Bible Translation

M ost nonfiction books have a preface. Whoever wrote that did so intending to convey personal thoughts to the reader that help give the book some context. A writer might recount how the book came about and what it was that prompted her to tackle the project in the first place. The writer might want to thank people who influenced the content or provided assistance of some kind toward its publication.

A preface differs from a chapter of introduction since the latter is usually considered part of the book's content. In other words, a preface doesn't contribute to the subject matter of the book, but it does provide important information for framing or appreciating the subject matter. In the case of a Bible translation, the preface explains how it was created and explains the publishing decisions on formatting and style.

For example, the preface to the ESV discusses its translation philosophy. The scholars who produced the ESV had as their aim a translation that was "essentially literal" and proceeds to explain that such an approach "seeks as far as possible to capture the precise wording of the original text and the personal style of each Bible writer." Consequently, "emphasis is on 'word-for-word' correspondence, at the same time taking into account differences of grammar, syntax, and idiom between current literary English and the original languages." There are in fact other approaches to translation, such as rendering the biblical text *thought-for-thought* instead of word-for-word, or preferring to paraphrase the text. For serious study of the biblical text, this is useful information, especially if you are dependent on English translations.

We also learn from the ESV's preface that, for the Old Testament, it occasionally departed from the traditional ("Masoretic") Hebrew text in favor of adopting a different wording from the Dead Sea Scrolls. Rather than insert a divergent reading from the Dead Sea Scrolls in a marginal footnote, the ESV puts the alternative wording in the actual running text of the translation. This is most clearly evident in Deuteronomy 32:8, 43. This information is also important for the Bible student. It offers a clear answer as to why the ESV translation would disagree with other English translations at certain points.

Before your next Bible study session, if you haven't already done so, read the preface to your translation. Don't skip it. You'll learn something you can use in your Bible study.

CHAPTER 29

There's No Such Thing as "Holy Ghost Greek"

The New Testament was originally written in Greek. Like every language, Greek changes over time in script, word meanings, and grammar. Contemporary spoken and written English has significant differences from English of prior eras. This is most easily seen in vocabulary. Fifty years ago words like "blog," "Facebook," and "chatroom" didn't exist in English. There are also differences, for example, between British and American English. So it should come as no surprise that the Greek of the New Testament is different than Greek of other periods.

These differences, along with the nature of the New Testament, led many people, including scholars, to suppose that the New Testament's Greek was special, perhaps even created by divine providence specifically to communicate the truth of the gospel. People took this idea seriously into the late 1800s. Today, it's known to be a complete falsehood.

The mythical nature of this belief was exposed in the late nineteenth and early twentieth centuries by archaeological discoveries of previously unknown Greek manuscripts. For example, toward the end of the nineteenth century, thousands of papyrus fragments written in Greek were discovered in Egypt in garbage dumps. Greek scholars quickly discerned that the Greek of these fragments was the same type of Greek found in the New Testament and the early church fathers, a stage of the language known as "common" Greek, or *koinē* Greek (pronounced, *koinay*).

Koine Greek is a byproduct of Alexander the Great's conquest. Although Alexander's soldiers were Greeks, they spoke different versions of the Greek language. There were numerous dialects. To effectively communicate with each other, a "common" form of the language was created and spread. As Alexander's armies swept east across the Mediterranean, Asia Minor (modern Turkey), Mesopotamia, and into India, this common Greek spread throughout his empire. This common (*koinē*) Greek is the language of the New Testament.

There is no such thing as "Holy Ghost Greek." We ought not assign any special status to it when we're doing word studies in our study of Scripture. Doing so leads to flawed interpretation. Fortunately, the Greek of the New Testament *wasn't* special. It was the Greek spoken and read throughout the known world. Consequently, the message of the New Testament was understood everywhere.

CHAPTER 30

Learn about Hebrew Poetic Parallelism

Don't worry. I'm not going to tell you that you need to learn Hebrew to do Bible study. (I'm admittedly biased in that direction, but I have to be honest).

There's a lot of poetry in the Old Testament. Hebrew poetry doesn't work like poetry as we think of it. The kind of poetry we're exposed to in school or maybe on greeting cards rhymes in *sound*:

> Mary had a little lamb. Its fleece was white as snow.
> And everywhere that Mary went the lamb was
> sure to go.

Hebrew poetry, on the other hand, rhymes in *thought*. That is, the second (or successive) line in Hebrew poetry will echo the first in some way. That's very handy to know for Bible study in books like Psalms and Proverbs. Modern English translations do a nice job of aligning Hebrew poetry in such a way that the English reader can tell what lines immediately relate to one another. If we can discern that with the eye, interpretation can proceed to how the lines are echoing each other. Scholars typically express this phenomenon with the advice, "Line A. . . . What's more, Line B." Line A says something; then line B elaborates. The only trick is that the thought-rhyming can be accomplished in a wide range of ways. Some examples will illustrate this.

Psalm 119:105 (A and B are synonymous thoughts)
　　A—Your word is a lamp to my feet,
　　B—and a light to my path.

Psalm 1:6 (B echoes A, but in opposite terms)
　　My son,
　　A—The Lord knows the way of the righteous,
　　B—but the way of the wicked will perish.

There are over a dozen options for understanding the relationships between lines of Hebrew poetry. The lines reinforce each other in thought. Parallelism helps us to see elements that are meant to be understood in tandem. Sometimes that's handy for word study—parallelism is a context for a word's usage. Having an eye for line relationships in poetry helps Bible students understand the biblical writer's intended idea and weed out unintended interpretations.

CHAPTER 31

The Books in Your Bible Are Not in Chronological Order

Have you ever wondered how historians know when things in the ancient world happened? How can we say with great confidence that some event happened 1,000 years before Christ (BC)? How do we know with precision when the events of the life of Jesus and the early Church transpired?

Ancient chronology is a fascinating subject. It's also amazingly complex since it deals not only with ancient lists of the reigns of kings that have survived from antiquity but also with ancient astronomical observations and their recording. You don't need to devote yourself to understanding *how* all these things are known in order to study the Bible. But it's pretty important you know the *when*.

The books in your Bible were not chronologically arranged. Ezekiel was not written after Jeremiah. Paul's epistles were not written in the order they're listed in the New Testament. Even books like 1–2 Samuel can be chronologically misleading. Samuel was the last of Israel's judges, right before the first king, Saul, came along. Consequently, the *content* of 1–2 Samuel overlaps Samuel's life and a time that followed the events of the Torah, Joshua, and Judges. But the *content* of a book doesn't tell us when a book was *written*. The fact that 1–2 Samuel never claim to have been written by Samuel adds to the chronological uncertainty.

Scholars have done their best to determine when the books of the Bible were actually written, but there's a lot of disagreement. Yet the effort is worth it because knowing when a book was written is important for the development of theological ideas. For example, what Paul says about faith and works in Galatians (perhaps his earliest epistle) sounds a bit different than it does in Romans. Paul's comments are specific to events in Galatians, whereas Romans reflects a fuller treatment of the issue, one that benefits from years of preaching and addressing the issue in churches.

Another reason to know when a book was written is that it provides a glimpse of the writer's world. Knowing that the Egyptians wrote about the invasion of the Sea Peoples (from whom the Philistines derive) along the coast of Canaan helps us put certain references to the Philistines in the Old Testament in context.

Fortunately, this sort of information is available in reference works and good commentaries. Taking time to get your chronological bearings helps interpretation.

CHAPTER 32

The Traditional Hebrew Text of the Old Testament Did Not Fall from Heaven

I've already talked a little about how Greek was not specially created by God for the New Testament. That myth was popular before the late nineteenth century, and it remains influential to this day. A similar myth claims that the traditional Hebrew Old Testament (the Masoretic text) deserves special sacred status. It doesn't, and being influenced by that idea can hinder your Bible study.

There are several tools that can help English readers with the original languages. Other tools guide English readers to what various manuscripts say that might diverge from something in their translation. Manuscript copies of the Hebrew Old Testament have slight variations, none of which affect central doctrines, and Bible translations will sometimes note these small wording changes. If you think the traditional Hebrew text is sacrosanct, these tools won't help you.

The myth claims that the Hebrew text hasn't changed since its original composition—that the ancient Jewish scribes, the Masoretes, didn't change a letter. The Dead Sea scrolls are often rolled out to make this argument. But it's a myth, and the scrolls themselves demonstrate that.

The problem with the myth is that the work of the Masoretes

only began around AD 100, when the Hebrew Bible (the Old Testament) was standardized by the Jewish religious authorities. There were various manuscripts of the Hebrew Bible in existence prior to that time. The most important one is the text from which the Septuagint, the Greek translation of the Old Testament, was created. The Septuagint was very popular with early Christians and, naturally, with the writers of the New Testament. It was popular because it was a Greek translation. However, the Hebrew text from which the Septuagint was translated and the text known today as the Masoretic text differ in some ways.

The rabbis wanted a standardized text for their community. So in AD 100 they took the existing texts and used them to produce a single text that would be copied down from that point on. That's the Masoretic text. The Dead Sea Scrolls preserve differences from other texts. Those other texts are where many of the marginal notes in your study Bible come from.

My point is this: don't be afraid to seriously entertain an alternative textual reading in your Bible's footnotes. You might be returning to the original reading.

CHAPTER 33

Learn Something about Philosophies of Bible Translation

Bible translation is both an art and a science. It's not just a matter of knowing English equivalents to words in the original Hebrew, Aramaic, and Greek. If you are bilingual or have a friend who speaks another language, you know there's more to understanding what is communicated in any language than using a dictionary.

The difficulty is easy to illustrate in English. Understanding what is meant by phrases liked "She copped a plea" or "He's piling up yards" requires cultural knowledge—in these cases, the slang of crime dramas and the nuances of football. We could translate those phrases word-for-word into another language but without the appropriate cultural intuition, they'd be meaningless.

Bible translators struggle with these sorts of problems frequently. There are also issues unique to the Bible that present difficulties. The doctrine of inspiration is one such complication. Since inspiration can be defined as "verbal," where each word of the original compositions is ultimately the result of a process guided by Providence, should translation of those compositions take the form of a "word-for-word" rendering? If not, are words of God being lost?

This "word-for-word" approach to translation is called "formal equivalence" by translators. The goal of this translation philosophy is to account for each word in the original language with an English word wherever that is possible. The result is typically a rigidly literal rendering that may sound awkward. But each word must be accounted for. Some Bible translations definitely lean this direction.

Another approach is called "dynamic equivalence" or "functional equivalence." This approach looks at the material to be translated and assesses what the original material meant to its original audience. Once that is discerned, the *meaning* is put into English using whatever words are best suited toward that end. There is no emphasis on accounting for each word of the original since *meaning* is the focus. Again, certain translations favor this approach.

Some translations fall in between. Still others are actually paraphrases. Paraphrases start with an English translation and then reword the English. No actual translation work occurs.

I like to say the best Bible translation is the one you'll read. It's good to know the philosophy behind your translation. Using several translations that take different approaches is actually useful for Bible study.

CHAPTER 34

Get to Know the Features of Your Study Bible

A lot of people have study Bibles. They are annually one of the bestselling items in Christian bookstores. It's a shame that most people who have one use only a fraction of what it offers. The problem isn't illiteracy. It's negligence.

The scholars and publishers who produce study Bibles put a great deal of thought into them. They are designed to facilitate Bible study and not just to be read like a novel or a newspaper. Study Bibles have a wide range of features to help people move beyond Bible reading.

All study Bibles include introductions to each book that discuss who wrote it and why. Knowing the circumstances that prompted the writing of the book is a crucial context for framing its contents.

Many study Bibles also include essays on important topics in a book, difficult or controversial passages, or the role the book plays in the bigger theological picture of the Bible. These sorts of essays orient readers to a book's contribution to doctrine and biblical history.

Some study Bibles employ their own system of symbols to draw the reader's attention to further information about words. If you're familiar with Strong's numbers, then you'll know that some study Bibles feature numbering systems with a concordance and brief Hebrew and Greek dictionaries to help readers get into word study.

A good study Bible will also come with "extras" like explanations of biblical chronology, timelines, a glossary for weights and measures, a history of how we got the Bible, reading plans, extended maps, charts, and—very important for Bible study—a well-conceived, detailed index.

But all these aids will be for naught unless you find them and use them. Don't treat your study Bible like it's a pew Bible, with nothing but the running English translation. It's so much more.

CHAPTER 35

Pay Attention to the Formatting of Your Bible Translation

No, I'm not recommending that you need a degree in book design for productive Bible study. I *am* recommending that you pay attention to how the biblical text is presented in your translation. Believe it or not, Bible publishers use specific formatting conventions to draw the reader's eye to features of the text that do indeed assist in Bible study.

Let's start with something every English Bible reader has seen but likely not considered: line breaks and indenting. Look at Psalm 1:1–2 in the ESV:

> Blessed is the man
> who walks not in the counsel of the wicked,
> nor stands in the way of sinners,
> nor sits in the seat of scoffers;
> but his delight is in the law of the LORD,
> and on his law he meditates day and night.

Notice how the formatting breaks the poem into stanzas, clearly showing which thoughts are in parallel to each other. Proper formatting is crucial for drawing attention to how Hebrew poetry works. Now look at the same passage in the 1769 edition of the King James Version:

> Blessed is the man that walketh not in the counsel of the
> ungodly, nor standeth in the way of sinners, nor sitteth in the
> seat of the scornful. But his delight is in the law of the LORD;
> and in his law doth he meditate day and night.

There is no formatting, no line breaks and indentation, to bring out the parallelisms. The text is presented as simple prose like historical narrative would be. The symmetry of the lines is completely lost.

Here's another example. Modern translations segment chapters into pericopes, sections of prose that the grammar of the original text marks off as thought units. Observing the pericope divisions helps Bible students discern the immediate context of a verse within that unit.

So, yes, formatting matters. Don't just read your Bible. Observe it.

CHAPTER 36

Font Style Matters

What difference could font style mean in your Bible study? You'd be surprised.

Let's talk about *italics*. Did you know that some English translations use italics to indicate words in the translation that have been supplied for the sake of English, but for which no word in the original language exists? For example, Genesis 1:2 reads as follows in many editions of the King James Version:

> And the earth was without form, and void; and darkness *was* upon the face of the deep.

The word "was" is in italics because there is no verb in the Hebrew original behind that English word. It's supplied for English smoothness. You'll want to be careful with any Bible interpretation that depends on italicized words.

Small capital letters are used in nearly every English translation, particularly with the name of God. Deuteronomy 6:4 in the ESV reads:

> Hear, O Israel: The LORD our God, the LORD is one.

Notice that the word "LORD" is spelled with small capital letters. This is a publishing convention to tell the reader that the Hebrew word being translated is the divine name, YHWH ("Yahweh"). This distinguishes the sacred name from the generic word for "lord, master" in Hebrew, *adon*. The Bible uses many names for God, and the presence (or absence) of the sacred name can make a difference in the interpretation of a passage.

On those occasions where the divine name and this more generic word occur in tandem, English Bible publishers render the combination as "Lord GOD." Genesis 15:2 is one such instance:

> But Abram said, "O Lord GOD ..."

The word *adon* is translated "Lord" with normal capitalization, and the divine name, YHWH, is rendered "GOD" with initial normal capital and the rest with small capitals. "Lord LORD" would just sound awkward.

The takeaway is that sometimes your translation is giving you information hidden in plain sight. Everything you see on the page has a decision behind it.

PART 3

ACCURATELY INTERPRET THE BIBLE

CHAPTER 37

Prayer Doesn't Guarantee Your Interpretation Is Accurate

God is not a vending machine. He is not the genie of all genies, in covenant with his people to grant their every wish. No mature Christian, of course, would ever think of God in such terms. We know that God does not always give us what we ask for in prayer. We trust that God has good reasons for such denials. Paul asked the Lord to rid him of the mysterious "thorn in the flesh" three times, but the answer was no (2 Cor. 12:7–10). Even Jesus was refused when he asked God to deliver him from death on the cross if it was God's will.

Upon reflection, this pill isn't so hard to swallow. Perhaps the thing we so desperately want wouldn't be good for us. Perhaps our motives aren't completely upright. Even if they are, perhaps God has something better planned. These reasons are hard to fathom, though, when we ask God to illumine our mind to understand Scripture. Why wouldn't God want *that*?

Of course God wants us to rightly understand the Bible. He desires our understanding like he desires us to treat our spouse kindly, tell someone the gospel, or meet someone's emotional or financial need when it's in our power to do so (Prov. 3:27). But all of these spiritual endeavors depend in part upon our own will, discernment, and ability. Bible study is no exception.

This is transparently obvious when you think about it. We know from their writings that Augustine, Aquinas, Luther, Calvin, and Wesley prayed that they would properly understand Scripture and believed God had answered that prayer. Yet these famous theologians came to dramatically different conclusions on many topics and in many passages. John Calvin, for example, is famous for his insistence that the salvation of individual believers was predestinated, an idea Wesley rejected. Luther's judgment that the book of James didn't belong in the New Testament would have drawn objections from the rest of these theologians.

While it's certainly appropriate to ask God to guide our study, it's our responsibility to develop skill and experience in studying Scripture. Prayer is no cover for either meager effort or failure to address our own inadequacies as students. Most Bible students accept that until they're in the heat of a theological joust or feel the urge to explain why their church is better than someone else's. Resist the temptation to believe that you prayed yourself correct or to say to yourself, "but for answered prayer, I might be mistaken." Hone your skills and ask God to help you do the best you can.

CHAPTER 38

All Interpretations Are Not Equally Plausible

It's time for a confession. I'm lethal to small group Bible studies. Honestly, I don't try to be. I don't sit there waiting to pounce on a defective interpretation. I pray for invisibility. Trust me, I'm not opposed to "normal folks" sharing their impressions about something they've read in the Bible. Scholars don't own that space. It does my heart good to see people engaged over Scripture, even if I know their conclusions are wide of the mark. But sooner or later somebody (usually my wife) notices I'm there and asks me what I think. Oh well. There's always another small group.

Offering my two cents is uncomfortable because I can't bring myself to be dishonest about Scripture. As a biblical scholar, I realize that the scriptural standard for truthfulness doesn't eliminate tact or compel exhaustive critique in this situation. But every effort at diplomacy seems to end in spilling the beans that not all interpretations are equally plausible. Whether others let on or not, I instinctively know that something I've said just consigned one or more viewpoints to the dustbin of defectiveness.

We're all wrong at some point in our understanding of Scripture. It's unavoidable. Yet I've seen this indisputable truth produce disconcerting responses.

For example, some people get defensive. They cherish their

viewpoint so much that it distorts clear thinking. Some people presume that since no human knows everything, any idea that exists is possible. Not true. The word "possible" is necessarily held in check by the word "plausible." They are not interchangeable. It strokes our ego to think we can do or be anything and that all our thoughts deserve careful consideration, but the truth is that we can't and they don't. Yes, I suppose it's *possible* that I could be an NFL quarterback next year. The year after that it's *possible* that I'll win a Grammy for my debut rap album. But these *possibilities* are so absurd that they are not at all *plausible*.

Other folks get discouraged if they're mistaken. This is more common. Don't let the inescapable reality of imperfection paralyze you from studying the Bible. As the saying goes (most often attributed to Voltaire), "The perfect is the enemy of the good." Good but imperfect Bible study is better than no Bible study. God doesn't expect perfection in our study of Scripture. He expects perseverance.

CHAPTER 39

Some Things in the Bible Are Clearer than Others—by Design

The Bible is an uneven book. If you think about the range of subjects it covers, some things just get a lot more attention than others. For example, the Bible has a lot more to say about Moses and the exodus from Egypt than what Moses did in Midian for forty years after fleeing from Pharaoh (Acts 7:29–30). Most of what the New Testament tells us about Jesus covers the final three and a half years of his life. We know nothing about Jesus from the time he was twelve (Luke 2:41–52) to the beginning of his ministry when he was around thirty (Luke 3:23).

The Bible's presentation of doctrine is the same way. We're told a great deal about the nature of salvation, the meaning of what Jesus did on the cross, the relationship of faith and works, and the work of the Holy Spirit. We're told next to nothing about where angels and demons come from or the origin of the soul.

The imbalance is deliberate. The biblical writers had agendas with respect to what they wrote. Their books come out of specific circumstances and target specific events or questions. It was God who prompted them to write when they did, and to do so from their sociocultural contexts. God chose specific men and specific times and places to write for spiritual posterity. God's choices are intelligent and deliberate. The very nature of the enterprise of inspiration means that the product—the Bible—will be selective.

Let's think about what this means and doesn't mean. I'm not suggesting that items to which the Bible devotes little space are unimportant. *Everything* the Bible comments on is important. Every passage in Scripture has some communicative purpose. What I'm saying is that frequency and repetition indicate emphasis. If we are mindful of inspiration as the providential process it was, frequency telegraphs that certain truths are more central to the overall biblical message.

The situation is sort of like a website. Most of your attention is drawn to big pictures or prose text. That's what holds your interest, *by design*. Tiny links are scattered here and there amid the prose, in the margins, across the top. They don't communicate much by themselves. But following them can illumine the whole point of the website. Both are indispensable.

CHAPTER 40

Don't Be Shaken by Your Lack of Omniscience

From time to time I get asked if I've ever changed my viewpoint on something in the Bible. People often presume that scholars have everything nailed down. We don't. I've always told my students the truth about that, and so I'll tell you. Of course I've changed my mind. That's what happens when people think, keep absorbing information, and are in the habit of asking God for the courage to be humble and theologically honest.

I know that a lot of people feel some anxiety about saying "I'm not sure right now" or "I changed my mind" when it comes to interpreting the Bible. Parents might fear doing so because they don't want their kids turning to other sources, such as their peers and the information maelstrom we call the internet. Scholars might feel uneasy about the admission since they're supposed to be authorities. Worrying accomplishes nothing in either case. Your kids are going to talk to their peers and search YouTube no matter how brilliant your answers are. And I'm sorry, professor, but your seminarians or graduate students know you don't know everything, so just deal with it.

Pastors have a unique hurdle in this regard. The people in the pew have a habit of presuming the pastor is an expert on the Bible and doctrine. They typically don't have access to biblical scholars and can rarely name one. In the eyes of their people, pastors are the default scholars. In view of that burden, I've known many pastors who are afraid to sound uncertain in front of their people. Not knowing what a passage means "for sure" or how to flawlessly unravel a theological knot might reveal a chink in the armor, or so they presume. This is unfortunate and unfair to those in ministry.

Even if you're not a pastor or seminarian, odds are high that if you are a serious student of Scripture, you also teach others or will be asked to do so at some point. When your students ask you questions, try to fix it in your mind and heart that they're not probing you for weaknesses. They're sincere. They want to know, and you're their best shot at getting an answer right now. Do your best, tell them when you're not sure, and then get busy finding the answer.

CHAPTER 41

Lots of Things in the Bible Can't Be Understood by Children

I rarely watch television. It's not because I have some pseudopious objection to it. For me it's a time issue, except when it comes to sitcoms. If I was confined to a bed, I wouldn't watch a sitcom. I used to love them as a teenager, probably for the same reasons I tend to dislike them now as a parent.

One of my irritations with the sitcom genre is how every adult is portrayed as a half-wit while the kids are endless sources of wisdom and clear-headed thinking. The only skills that mom and dad seem to have are getting into trouble and being smart enough to let their kids extricate them from their problems.

Maybe this is why one of my pet peeves is the notion that the Bible is so simple even a child can understand it. Don't get the wrong idea—I know that the gospel story of Jesus really can be understood at a young age. But I'm talking about more than the gospel. As someone who has taught a lot in the local church and in the classroom, I've heard the expression stated as a duty simply to avoid thinking. "I just want to love Jesus. Why are you complicating things?" I want to love Jesus too. Why are you being lazy about knowing God's Word?

Serious Bible study is work. It can be tedious at times. It doesn't always provide an immediate payoff in terms of addressing a spiritual struggle or answering a knotty question. Teddy Roosevelt once said, "Nothing in the world is worth having or worth doing unless it means effort, pain, difficulty. . . . I have never in my life envied a human being who led an easy life. I have envied a great many people who led difficult lives and led them well." Amen. I've never wanted to emulate anyone who halted their study of Scripture with what their kids knew. I've sought to be like those who put real effort and sacrifice into the enterprise.

As Art Linkletter used to remind television audiences, "Kids say the darnedest things." They sure do, but I'm not expecting to hear one explain why God told Samuel to deceive Saul's men (1 Sam. 16:1–5), or what Paul was thinking when he talked about baptism for the dead (1 Cor. 15:29), or a long list of other things in the Bible. Discovering those answers is for adults.

CHAPTER 42

Don't Ignore Footnotes

D o you remember learning to read? I have a vague recollection from first grade of learning how to sound out letters for reading. Even if you can't remember learning yourself, chances are you've listened to a small child who is learning to read sound out the words. Perhaps even helped that child learn.

Children's storybooks follow typical patterns, patterns that persist through early grade school years. Simple one- or two-syllable words predominate. Sentences are very short. There are colorful pictures illustrating the points of the story. These things would be out of place in a book intended for an adult reader. In fact, we tend to judge intelligence by the absence of these things. Granted, there are exceptions, but books with short words and pictures tend to be for kids.

One of the arbiters for nonfiction adult material is the use of footnotes or end notes. We usually encounter those sorts of books in high school or college. The inclusion of footnotes presumes that the reader is not reading for casual interest but for *study*. This underlying assumption is also behind the inclusion of marginal notes in a Bible or longer notes that accompany the English translation. This is the common feature of all *study* Bibles. Following these notes to where they lead and reading that material is one strategy for moving beyond reading into Bible study.

There are three reasons why academic writers use footnotes.

If this were a quiz, I'm betting most people would get this one: writers want to tell you where they found some piece of information. They want to credit their source. Another reason is that a writer has a parenthetical thought that he or she feels might interrupt the discussion if it were added. A footnote allows a writer to include that extra thought without interrupting the flow of what's being said. A third reason is to direct readers to additional information or resources. This goes beyond crediting a source. The writer wants the reader to know that there are some excellent resources that will add to the discussion or maybe bolster a point being made. The assumption is that people who want to learn will follow the leads.

Footnotes and other notes *direct* the good student toward greater progress. Don't turn down help when it's offered.

CHAPTER 43

Context Is King

We spend a lot of time talking about interpreting the Bible in context. But truth be told, the Bible is often interpreted out of context in some way. I'm not exaggerating. When you know what's meant by "context," it's hard to think otherwise.

When most Bible-believers hear someone insist the Bible be interpreted in context, they usually presume the point is that whatever verse or verses they're reading or the pastor is preaching about need to be interpreted in light of the verses that precede and follow. While that's true, the verses before and after are just *one* context that needs consideration. Every biblical passage has *multiple* contexts. There is never just one context for interpreting the Bible.

The *worldview* of the biblical writers is a fundamentally important context in which the Bible must be interpreted if it is to be accurately understood. The proper worldview context for interpreting the Bible is not evangelicalism, Catholicism, the Protestant Reformation, the Puritans, or even the modern world. The proper context for interpreting the Bible is the context in which it was written—that of the ancient biblical writers. Every other worldview is foreign to the Bible. This means we must do our best to think as the writers thought.

Another context for interpretation is *literary* context or genre. A genre is a type of literature. Frankly, without knowing the genre, accurate interpretation of word meaning is impossible. For example, if we saw the word "descent" in a document, it would matter a lot if that document were a genealogy, a landscape architect's plan, a flight instructor's manual, or a doctor's note about a grave illness. Those are all genres—kinds of writing. It's easy to see how they dictate meaning. Just as today, there were many different genres used in the Bible by the writers.

Lastly, every word has its own context in relationship to other words. If you look it up in a dictionary, the word "run" has dozens of meanings. It can be a verb or a noun. We only know what part of speech it is when we see the other words around it in a sentence. That knowledge, along with other contexts, helps us comprehend the intended meaning.

All of the above and more is why I like to say we need to interpret the Bible in contexts. There's more than one, and, collectively, context is king.

CHAPTER 44

Impressions Are No Substitute for Data

G ood Bible study should affect the way we think and feel. Naturally, the process of discovery in Bible study will appeal to the intellect because we learned something. But there's more to the life of the mind than the accumulation of facts. There are other things going on inside our heads besides information storage. Our emotions, attitudes, and imaginings are just as much part of our internal life as processing power.

All the aspects of our thought life need to be informed by good data, that is, things that are true and correct. Without real facts, our feelings, beliefs, and actions can be prompted by flawed catalysts. In the case of the Bible, truths that mold us in all these ways must derive from the biblical text. They cannot be the result of impressions or suspicions about something that might be biblical.

Bible studies can easily be derailed by putting impressions on equal (or superior) footing with data drawn from the biblical text. Attempts to calculate the return of Jesus are a good example of this. The biblical text clearly tells us that no one knows the "day and hour" of the Lord's return (Matt. 24:36), but that hasn't stopped a lot of Bible teachers and students from thinking otherwise.

I've had a lot of strange ideas come across my desk that can be filed under "interpretation by impression." I'm convinced that cable television is the root cause for most of them. Asteroids have hit the earth in the past—I wonder if that's what caused the flood? Parts of the desert have been irrigated in Israel—I'll bet that has something to do with prophecy about Israel.

Speculating, especially about antiquity, is fun. I enjoy it as much as the next person. But the serious Bible student must clearly distinguish between speculation and exegesis. The latter is the domain of the biblical text. The former is not. What you believe can be either coherently traced to the text or not. Building aptitude in Bible study will keep you oriented to that standard.

CHAPTER 45

Words Don't Mean Anything by Themselves

We all know from experience that the words we use can be understood and intended in different ways. No word means the same exact thing every time it's used. I love my wife and I love pizza. The pizza really isn't giving my wife competition for my attention. My emotional attachment to my wife is of a different nature and intensity than my desire for pizza. But I can use the word "love" with respect to both.

What helps us so easily parse a difference here? Real life. Our experiences provide context. Words don't mean anything in isolation. They *can't* mean anything until they are put in context. Context determines word meaning; nothing else does.

For some reason, this obvious truth gets lost for some Bible students who are doing word studies. The process goes something like this: Research tools help us identify the original language word behind an English word that draws our interest in a particular verse. Then we look up that word in a word study dictionary. So far so good. But here's where many Bible students go off the tracks. All too often, students use these dictionaries to discover what a Greek or Hebrew word can mean, to latch on to an interesting option, and to mine for verses where the word has the meaning we're looking for. The fact that the word *can* have a given meaning, and actually does in other verses, provides a justification for assigning that meaning to the word in the verse under scrutiny.

That isn't word study. That's cherry-picking a meaning from a list of possibilities and considering *other* contexts (other verses) in place of the context of the word in your passage. Seeing that clearly should remind us that a word's meaning in one instance may be different in another.

Real word studies take time. There is no substitute for discerning the contexts that come to bear on the word you want to study and then, one by one, testing whether other meanings are possible in that same setting. Context makes that determination, not a list of possible meanings in a dictionary.

CHAPTER 46

Don't Confuse Correlation with Causation

Have you ever seen those commercials that string a series of disastrous events together which lead to how buying their product will save you from all the disasters? They're funny because they exploit connections between seemingly random, unrelated events just to steer you toward a conclusion. As if not liking my haircut will lead to a typhoon. These commercials use *non sequiturs* (conclusions which do not logically follow) to make us laugh and remember a product. In that sense, they're effective.

One of the most common logical fallacies is the confusion of correlation with causation. The fallacy is presuming that two things that are related somehow—perhaps by timing, or similarity of appearance or theme—must mean that one causes or leads to the other. Whether you've had a formal course in logic or not, you've encountered this one. You can literally find examples of it every day in newspapers, blogs, and of course commercials. I ran across one today: a television report dutifully told viewers about the "interesting fact" that as the shoe sizes of elementary kids increase, so do scores on standardized reading exams. Sure, both studies run at the same time and even on the same kids have a correlation, but did one really cause the other? Should I despair if my child has small feet? "Sally will never be able to read well unless her feet grow." I hope you see the error in this thinking.

Confusing correlation and causation can be comical, but when it shows up in sermons, Sunday school lessons, and Bible study resources, it isn't funny. Even doctrinal beliefs can derive from this logical fallacy. One example that I've seen repeatedly is the belief that there was a rebellion of one-third of the angels in heaven prior to the fall, which in turn explains the temptation in Eden. The Bible nowhere teaches such a cause-and-effect. A rebellion of one-third of the angels occurs in Revelation 12:1–9, where it is clearly connected to the first coming of Jesus and his resurrection (Rev. 12:5), not Eden. But since Revelation 12:9 mentions the serpent, there is some sort of correlation intended. But very obviously this rebellion did not precipitate Genesis 3 and the fall.

The point should be clear: we must pause and think carefully about any claim we run across, or pops into our minds, in order to avoid this fallacy.

CHAPTER 47

What Is Meant by "Literal" Interpretation of the Bible Needs Interpretation

Many readers have heard the old bromide in defense of literal Bible interpretation: "When the plain sense makes sense, seek no other sense." It's pithy. If you don't think too much about it, it might even sound like it makes sense. It's actually not very helpful.

Consider the word "water." What does it "literally" mean? What exactly is its "plain sense"? Here are a few possibilities:

Noun:
- H_2O (chemical compound)
- Body of water ("Look at all that water.")
  - Ocean
  - Sea
  - Lake
  - Pond
  - River
  - Stream
  - Creek
  - Inlet
- Liquid drink ("I'd like some water.")
- Hydration supply ("They turned off the water.")

Verb:

- Irrigate ("Water the fields.")
- Provide hydration ("He watered the cattle.")
- Saliva ("My mouth watered.")
- Tearing up ("His eyes watered.")

Which one of these is the plainest of the plain? That's the point. They're *all* plain. What distinguishes them is context. Things get even more interesting when you move into metaphorical meanings for water, which can be exactly what context requires. "Water" can speak of a life source, purification, transformation, motion, or danger. The metaphors work because of the "literal" characteristics of water.

Biblical writers used words loaded with symbolic, abstract meanings that were well known in *their* culture. We miss all that when we insist words must mean what pops into *our* heads in our time and culture. What we ought to be trying to discern is what the biblical writers and their original readers were thinking, not what we're thinking. What the "plain sense" is to us may not have been at all plain to them.

CHAPTER 48

The Meaning of an Original Language Word Is Not Determined by the Sound of That Word in a Different Language

I know what you're thinking. You're wondering how in the world anyone could think that what I'm denying above could be true. I agree; the idea is truly bizarre. That's why it's so disturbing when you encounter people who think they're "digging into the Word" by interpreting Scripture that way.

I'll start with a common example many readers will (sadly) have heard. Ezekiel 38:2–3 refer to a figure known as "Gog, chief prince of Meshech and Tubal." The Hebrew behind "chief prince" is pronounced *nesi rosh*. Some well-meaning Bible teachers want to translate the phrase "prince of Rosh" as though *rosh* is a proper noun of geography (it isn't). They observe that "Rosh" sounds a lot like "Russia," and "Meshech" and "Tubal" sound like "Moscow" and "Tobolsk," cities in Russia. Surely, then, Gog must be an enemy (perhaps even the antichrist) from Russia.

Stop laughing. I've seen that in print. More than once. It's absolute nonsense.

Simply put, languages just don't work this way. The fact that there is a Chinese word that sounds like *chin* doesn't mean that word describes a protrusion on the lower part of the face just under the lips. It doesn't. Not even close. The Hebrew word *dor* is not something with hinges that opens and closes. (The word means "generation"). Spanish *plata* does not mean "plate" (it means "silver, money"). The French verb *blesser* means "to wound, injure, or offend," not "invoke divine care" or "confer prosperity."

I could go on and on. The human mouth, tongue, teeth, and nose—the body parts responsible for making sounds as air moves through them from the lungs—are only capable of making a finite number of sounds. Every language on earth has arisen as people used those body parts to make sounds to communicate with each other. No language assigns the same meanings to all, or even most, of the same sounds. Few things in life could be more obvious.

Unfortunately, I've known authors, teachers, pastors, and Bible students that somehow miss something this palpably evident. Don't be misled. Word meaning depends on context, not sounds.

CHAPTER 49

"Level of Detail" Is Not a Key to Bible Interpretation

I'll have to explain this one. It's a pet peeve of mine.

The "level of detail" approach to interpretation is something that careless Bible teachers and even scholars use to justify certain "literal" interpretations of prophecy, whatever "literal" means. The more detailed an Old Testament prophecy (so we are told), the more it demands a literal fulfillment in the "end times."

Really? Let's think about that logic.

More detail in a prophecy = literal interpretation. If so, what does that mean for prophecies that have less detail? Should we presume their fulfillment is nonliteral? The truth is that the amount of words or the length of a prophecy is no indication of how it should be interpreted.

For example, the prophet Ezekiel uses nine chapters (40–48) to envision a future, idealized temple that would replace the recently destroyed Jerusalem temple. The densely detailed description is often used to justify the interpretation that the vision requires a literal fulfillment—that Ezekiel's vision is the blueprint for a structure that will someday be built in Jerusalem. Other interpreters point out that the level of detail omits items that are crucial to a functioning temple. The prophecy is almost completely devoid of height dimensions, an odd omission if these were building plans.

Important furnishings found in the earlier temple and the tabernacle, such as the ark of the covenant and the golden lampstand, are missing from Ezekiel's description. There are no lavers for priests to wash themselves. There is no wall around the inner court and no roof to any part of the envisioned temple, which are both essential to preserve the sanctity of the sacred space. While nine chapters offer a great amount of detail, these omissions would produce an incomplete, nonfunctional building. Detail alone cannot justify literal interpretation.

Alternatively, prophecies of little more than one line were certainly envisioning a literal event. But that often didn't matter. They were still difficult. Even after the resurrection the disciples had trouble processing what had just happened and what it meant (Luke 24:36-49). The risen Jesus had to "open their minds to understand the Scriptures" (Luke 24:45). The Gospels were written in hindsight, and only in hindsight could the disciples discern the importance of prophecies like Zechariah 9:9 ("your king is coming to you . . . humble and mounted on a donkey"; cf. Matt. 21:5), Psalm 41:9 ("my close friend in whom I trusted, who ate my bread, has lifted his heel against me"; cf. John 13:38), and Psalm 78:2 ("I will open my mouth in a parable"; cf. Matt 13:35).

The point is that level of detail isn't a hermeneutical method for interpreting prophecy. This is especially true when the New Testament itself gives us an interpretation. At times, these New Testament interpretations defy any sort of literalism. Prophecy gets fulfilled in a *variety* of ways. But that's for another day.

CHAPTER 50

The Proper Context for Interpreting the Bible Is the Context That Produced the Bible

We often hear the mantra "interpret the Bible in context." But what that means can be easily misunderstood. Positively, there is more than one context that needs consideration for Bible interpretation. But the negative aspect of context is also important. By "negative" I mean interpreting the Bible through the lens of a context alien to the biblical writers.

Biblical theology must derive from the biblical text. That makes getting the whole "context" thing right.

The context for correctly understanding the Bible are not the writings of the early church fathers, men like Augustine, Irenaeus, and Tertullian. It is not the Catholic Church, despite the brilliance of theologians like Aquinas. It is not Reformation thought, the works of Luther, Calvin, and Zwingli. It is not the Puritans, the Wesley brothers, or the famous Princeton theologians like Warfield, Machen, and Wilson. It is not evangelicalism. The proper context for interpreting the Bible is the context that produced it. Every other context is a foreign context.

While this seems quite obvious, it is a truth frequently not observed in real life—and real Bible interpretation, preaching, and teaching. Filtering the Bible through writers, creeds, and confessions happens every day. It is the biblical text that's inspired, not these other leaders and their writings. If we fail to observe this truth, we'll end up in interpretive places that the inspired writers of the Bible never intended.

This is not to say historic Christianity got everything wrong. That would be a silly exaggeration. My point is one of priority and perspective. Bible interpretation that arose after the biblical period must take a back seat to the Bible itself. We must allow the world in which the biblical writers lived—their intellectual and cultural circumstances—to inform us about what the biblical authors wrote, how they wrote it, and why they wrote it. Only then will we be able to see the Bible like the original audience saw it. Only then can we avoid imposing a foreign context on our Bible interpretation.

CHAPTER 51

Most Passages in the Bible Don't Have Three Points to Communicate

I'll admit it. I'm taking a swipe at contemporary preaching. I'm in a curmudgeonly mood. But it's not just for personal satisfaction. It'll illustrate something important for Bible study.

Honest.

I can recall as a Bible college student marveling at preachers' ability to produce three points from any biblical passage. It didn't matter how short or long the passage was: three points. You could throw Zephaniah or Obadiah at them: three points. I've heard three-point sermons on *one verse*.

As a young pastoral intern required to preach for the pastors each week, I can recall casting aside passages in my Bible that I thought were really fascinating or spiritually challenging because I wasn't clever enough to break it down into three points. I didn't see the inspired symmetry. (Okay, that's a little over the top, but it felt good.)

It dawned on me one day that the problem wasn't me. It was the artificial nature of what I was trying to do. The goal of Bible study should be to grasp the meaning of the text. Serious study of the Bible should produce people who can trace the argument of the text or follow a theological breadcrumb trail through a book or section of the Bible. Working in a text means discerning *its* literary structure, intelligently created by the original authors to communicate to an audience that would have seen what they were doing.

If that sounds like work, it is. If you don't think Bible study is work, you aren't doing it. Serious Bible study requires spending time in the original text and learning the art of reading the Scripture as literature, *because that's what it is*. Biblical writers did not work without agendas or strategies. Their work isn't random. They were careful and deliberate about what they were writing. Inspiration isn't a synonym for amateur hour.

If the goal of Bible study is grasping the meaning of the text, the goal of preaching ought to be communicating that meaning. But all too often what happens in the pulpit isn't preaching the text—it's talking *about* the text. Any Bible student who has occasion to communicate their discoveries to someone else needs to know those enterprises are not the same. One is teaching the text. The other is transmitting your thoughts—in three points—about the text. Give me the former any day.

CHAPTER 52

The Meaning of a Word Does Not Come from Its Constituent Parts

Word studies are an important part of Bible study. Unfortunately, there's a lot of confusion about word meaning. Over the course of my Christian experience, I've encountered hundreds of flawed conclusions about what a word means in this or that passage.

One of the most common word study fallacies is the presumption that a word's "real" meaning can be discerned by breaking it into constituent parts. Greek sometimes allows this approach. Certain Greek verbs (e.g., *kaleo*, "to call") can have prepositions (e.g., *ek*, "out of, from") appended to them to form a single word (e.g., *ekkaleo*, "to call out"). A scholarly Greek-English dictionary (often called a lexicon) will help you to discern legitimate instances when this happens. You don't need to know Greek to use such tools if you are using a reverse interlinear. Biblical Hebrew words do not work this way at all.

It is generally best to avoid the approach altogether. Most words in any language do not mean what their parts mean. For example, words in English like "butterfly" and "quarterback" do not "really" mean that butter flies or that we're going to get change. Most words in any given language simply don't work this way. Approaching word studies as though they do is not only unreliable, but can be quite misleading.

125

The one consistent rule of word study is that word meaning is determined by an author's context. There's no shortcut for observing words in context if you want to understand what a biblical writer meant to say.

CHAPTER 53

Nonliteral Doesn't Mean "Not Real"

I talked earlier about how "literal" interpretation isn't easy to define. The whole idea of what "literal" interpretation means needs interpretation. The frequent insistence on thinking only in literal terms (whatever that means) has led to the caricature of other kinds of interpretation. Nonliteral interpretation, many are told, is just a strategy to avoid what the Bible clearly says. When something in the Bible threatens people (read: makes them draw a different conclusion than the one they favor), those panicked souls resort to "allegorizing" or "spiritualizing" the text.

That's nonsense.

I'm not denying that people do come up with weird interpretations to avoid something they don't like in Scripture. I'm denying that this is an acceptable portrayal of nonliteral interpretation. It had better be, since New Testament writers do at times take their Old Testament nonliterally.

The myth is that "nonliteral" somehow means "not real" or "I don't want what I'm reading to be real." The kind of nonliteral interpretation the New Testament writers sometimes engage in is hardly the result of wishing something in the Bible isn't true.

The idea behind the kind of nonliteral interpretation you'll find in the Bible is that sometimes the meaning of the text transcends what *we* would expect the passage to "literally" mean. The text means *more* than what immediately pops into our head. Nonliteral interpretation presumes that what God means by a statement might go beyond what humans presume. Since the spiritual realm is just as real as our physical, embodied existence, we have no right to make such presumptions. Nonliteral doesn't mean not real. It often means *more* real than you imagined.

For example, there is a considerable debate over the nature of the Antichrist figure in the New Testament. Some say the Antichrist will be a man, perhaps the Devil incarnate. Other say that Antichrist is a symbol of evil. In both perspectives the suffering of believers that ensues from the appearance of this man/evil is real. It would be dishonest for the "literal man" perspective to argue that the "symbol of evil" side wants to escape what the text says. Whatever the text means, the evil will be a clear and present danger.

Don't embrace caricatures of interpretive approaches you don't like or have little experience with. Find out what an approach really says.

CHAPTER 54

Be Open to Nonliteral Interpretation—the Biblical Writers Used It on Occasion

I just made the point that "nonliteral" doesn't mean "not real." In fact, when that interpretive approach happens in the New Testament, the meaning of a passage goes beyond a mundane "literal" expectation.

One of the more dramatic examples of a more-than-literal interpretation is what Luke does with a prophecy in Amos. In Amos 9:11–12, a prophecy about a time far distant to the prophet himself, God says through Amos:

> In that day I will raise up
> the booth of David that is fallen
> and repair its breaches,
> and raise up its ruins
> and rebuild it as in the days of old,
> that they may possess the remnant of Edom
> and all the nations who are called by my name.

On the surface—literally, one might say—the prophecy seems to be about repairing a physical structure, perhaps a tent booth (Deut. 16:13–16) or a wall. The purpose of this restoration is that

129

"they" may possess the remnant of Edom and all the nations called by God's name. The identity of "they" isn't specified, but given the history of Edom, one expects Israel is the one who will possess Edom. That creates the possibility that the "booth" of David may be metaphorical for David's dynasty.

Luke doesn't see any of that in Acts 15. In that chapter Peter relates the vision (Acts 10) God showed him about the message of salvation being for Gentiles, not Jews only. Right after that, when the apostle James hears about Paul's new ministry to the Gentiles, he sees what God has accomplished through Peter and Paul as the fulfillment of Amos 9! Luke writes:

> With this the words of the prophets agree, just as it is written,
> "After this I will return, and I will rebuild the tent of David
> that has fallen; . . . that the remnant of mankind may seek
> the Lord, and all the Gentiles who are called by my name."
> (Acts 15:15–17)

Luke (and James) don't balk at accepting a dramatically abstracted interpretation (Edom becomes "mankind," and "nations" is made the more specific "Gentiles"). This is quite different than what one would "literally" expect as a prophetic outcome, but it is quite real since the gospel was truly for everyone. When we study Scripture, we need to be open to other passages, especially those involving prophecy, working this way too.

CHAPTER 55

Total Objectivity in Bible Interpretation Is a Myth

Everybody likes to think they're objective. We all like to think we're capable of rendering opinions or judgments completely divorced from any external influence or personal bias. We don't like the suspicion that we've failed to weigh all possibilities about what a passage might mean before landing somewhere. That would make it seem like our position on some point of interpretation is somehow premature, careless, or unfair. We can cherish the thought, but it's a delusion.

Absolute objectivity about anything we enjoy thinking about or are forced to consider is an impossible standard. We can't hope to completely jettison every past sight, conversation, or experience from our minds that might nudge our opinions in a particular direction. Even if we're thinking about something or someone with which we have no prior experience, we have our own presuppositions. We weren't born with those. They are the cumulative result of all our life experiences, especially how we were raised as children.

Scholars aren't immune to this struggle. I recall one day in graduate school our professor lapsed into a mini-lecture on what it meant to be a scholar. One of his points was that "real" scholars approach the Bible with no biases or presumptions. Specifically, they bring no prior belief about the Bible to their analysis of the biblical text. Ideas like inspiration and anything else "confessional" had to be eliminated for real scholarship to occur.

I appreciated the spirit of the advice. We ought not filter what we see in the text through any theological grid. But I also had to shake my head. Absence of any religious or theological thought about the Bible is not only impossible but is *itself* a theological statement. The intellectual denial of the idea of inspiration (however defined) will indeed influence the way we process the data we glean from the text.

The honest thing to do is to acknowledge the beliefs we have. Every Bible student needs to own up to the fact that they might "believe" something only because the thought was handed down to them. Being up front with that possibility and letting people know we're trying hard to not filter the Bible through our beliefs fosters accountability. We shouldn't pretend we're immune from the experience we've acquired through past study or our interaction with others interested in the Bible. That's a façade.

CHAPTER 56

If It's Weird, It's Important

One of my pet peeves with preaching and Bible teaching in church is the propensity to skip odd or difficult passages in the Bible. This happens for several reasons.

Sometimes the person tasked with presenting Scripture presumes that the only passages truly "relevant" for folks in the pew are those that have some transparent point of application to life. That's usually the byproduct of poor Bible study, which in turn is often due to laziness. Passages that give us something to say after only a surface reading are good fodder for sermons.

At other times fear of getting the interpretation wrong encourages pastors or teachers to bypass a passage. Some passages appear to have no coherent explanation and application. I understand that one, but you shouldn't believe it. The solution involves a combination of the right tools and tenacity. Diligence is the friend, not the enemy, of the Bible student. It may take weeks, months, or longer to feel like you have a handle on a passage, but that shouldn't matter.

Still another reason is fear of discovery. For some Bible students, digging too deep into a passage might result in surrendering a belief they cherish. In my experience, this is more common than one would suppose. Fear of discovering something they believe may not be true prompts them to study something else.

Lastly, I've met all too many Bible students who don't want to think about certain passages because they are "too weird."

Surprisingly, this fear-based response often concerns ideas the Bible affirms that are uncomfortable in a modern world. If the passage turns out to mean what it seems to say, it wouldn't be rational. This fear is very inconsistent, especially since some of the things Christians believe are far from what someone who dismisses the supernatural would consider rational.

I'm not suggesting that we can always be certain we're interpreting strange or obtuse passages correctly. None of us is omniscient. Rather, my contention is that every passage in Scripture merits our attention. In many instances, the strange and difficult passages are part of a greater idea that is theologically significant. We just don't see it because we don't share the writer's ancient worldview. In my experience, if it's weird, it's important—there is a purpose for every passage in the Bible. It's our job to discover what it is.

CHAPTER 57

You Can't Understand the Bible Without Understanding the Worldview of the People Who Wrote It

I've talked before about the importance of context for interpretation. The context of the Bible involves many things. Think about the many contexts for anything we write. Our past and present experiences naturally color the way we look at the world. What enters our minds in various forms of media becomes part of how we intellectually process the world. How we were taught to express ourselves informs how we communicate. We are a product of the intellectual climate and resources that we absorb. So were the biblical writers.

A lot of what we find in the Bible cannot be understood well (or even at all) unless we see what's written through ancient eyes. We must be able to think like the ancient writer. Doing that requires sharing his worldview. Obviously, we can't hope to completely accomplish that task. But we providentially live at a time where it's more possible than ever to get inside the head of biblical writers with respect to their worldview.

The key to discovering the worldview of the biblical writers is to read material that reflects their time and culture. Archaeology has uncovered a large amount of the intellectual output of the cultures that were part of the biblical world. Numerous tablets and manuscripts have been translated into English. That makes it possible for us to think more like they did. We can not only read about what people from Egypt, Babylon, and Canaan wrote and thought, we can read that material ourselves.

There are some outstanding resources that help us navigate this terrain. The best starting points are two books, *Ancient Texts for the Study of the Hebrew Bible* and *Ancient Texts for New Testament Studies*. Both volumes are guides to the background literature produced by the civilizations of the ancient biblical world. The nine-volume *Zondervan Illustrated Bible Background Commentary* is also a premium reference tool.

Among the many resources these titles will direct you to are anthologies—collections of ancient texts in English translation. The most up-to-date scholarly set is the three-volume *Context of Scripture*. James Pritchard's *Ancient Near Eastern Texts Relating to the Old Testament* is a one-volume anthology. Other volumes focus solely on one writer or collection, such as the Dead Sea Scrolls, Josephus, or Philo. Access to the thinking of the ancient biblical world has never been more widely available.

CHAPTER 58

What a Word Meant before the Writer Lived Isn't an Indicator of What It Meant to the Writer

Word study is one of the most common Bible study strategies for folks who have moved beyond merely reading the Bible. The goal of word study is to penetrate your Bible translation to detect the words used by the authors in the original biblical languages. Strong's numbers are one strategy for doing that. Once you know the original language word, the goal is to discern whether the translator chose the best meaning from among the possible senses the word might have. Dictionaries of words in the biblical languages (lexicons) help Bible students with that task.

Word study is far more than looking up words in original language dictionaries. The effort has many pitfalls. One of the most common is the notion that what a word meant "originally" (when it first became part of the language) or in its most ancient usage somehow is the "real" meaning of that word. Such thinking is flawed.

Consider the word "monotheism," a word we understand as denoting the existence of only one God. That isn't what the word originally meant. The word "monotheism" first appeared in English in 1660 as an antonym for "atheism." So, originally, "monotheism" meant the belief in God as opposed to the rejection of that belief.

The original meaning of "monotheism" really doesn't lend itself to the way we think about the word today. In our time, we'd use "monotheism" in a discussion about polytheism, not about atheism.

The meaning of a biblical word might change with time. For example, the Hebrew word *ger* can refer to a foreigner, a resident alien, or a sojourner (a traveler). The correct nuance depends on the historical circumstances of the Old Testament book in which it is found. If the book was written at a time when Israel was a nation with its own land, then the first two options are viable. If not, then the third option is more likely. The circumstance of its occurrence in one book of the Bible really doesn't say anything about its meaning elsewhere.

Once again, context is king. Word meaning does not derive from the chronology of its usage. Word meaning is driven by current contexts, such as the type of literature in which the word appears (genre) or the writer's circumstances, which help us know if the usage might be metaphorical instead of literal.

CHAPTER 59

A Word Never Simultaneously Means All the Things It Can Mean

Words rarely mean only one thing. Most words in a given language can convey several senses. For example, the word "top" can refer to a garment worn on the upper body, the highest point of reference, or (as a verb) to cover or be superior to something. The right meaning depends on how the word is used in context.

It would be silly to suggest that the occurrence of the word "top" in any given sentence has all those meanings in that sentence. For instance, in the sentence "She was at the top of her field," do I mean to suggest that the woman "covered" a field so well that she "gained superiority" over everyone else and that her job happened to be in the highest floor of her office building, which housed a business that made clothing to be worn on the upper body? Of course not. The idea is as absurd as the illustration.

Naturally, I'd agree. The whole approach is comical. And yet I've seen it in Bible study notes, student papers, blog posts, and Bible-related articles submitted for publication. For some reason, people seem to believe that "Bible words" have some sort of mystical quality that allows us to throw out common sense when doing word studies. Just because a book is sacred doesn't mean its content must violate what makes a language coherent. Sanctified absurdity would still be absurdity.

No vocabulary of a language includes all possible meanings in every instance of usage. If you tell someone your wife is fetching, you mean she's attractive, not the obvious alternative that just popped into your head. If your kids are spoiled, you *don't* mean they are no longer edible.

This feature of language doesn't change when we come to the Bible. A biblical word that has a half-dozen senses doesn't bring them all into a verse at the same time. Hebrew and Greek words aren't like the heads of dandelions, waiting to release thousands of meanings into the air when held up to the wind.

The fact that God was providentially behind the production of Scripture doesn't change what he asked the human authors to do. They produced comprehensible documents, not literary onions that only elite mystics could unpeel and decipher. If Scripture failed to communicate to the masses, the entire enterprise would be pointless.

CHAPTER 60

Genre Is Another Word for Context

The first time I heard the term "literary genre" was in a high school English class. I didn't really like English lit, mostly for shallow reasons. It was too modern. I had a one-track mind for antiquity. If it wasn't written "BC," I really didn't care. I also thought it sounded too artsy and highbrowed. I was under the misguided notion that all I needed to do to understand the Bible was to be able to read. Genre seemed to be nothing more than a fancy term to confuse the simple act of reading.

What a dim bulb I was.

Fortunately, I had some good professors in seminary and graduate school that helped me get a firm grasp of the obvious. They taught me that it was absurd to talk about interpreting the Bible in context and throw genre to the wind. Genre *is* context (at least one of them).

To speak of literary genre is to speak of how any given piece of writing should be characterized in everyday life. Genre is how we describe a type of written document. In modern terms, all the following are examples of genres: email, blog posts, letters, receipts, contracts, poems, certificates, tax forms, wills, fiction, and non-fiction. Many of these can be categorized even more precisely. For example, fiction might include horror, sci-fi, comedy, history, suspense, mystery, and so on.

Genre is crucial for context because the same word occurring across different types of literature or documents will be understood quite differently. Why? Because genre dictates the perspective for interpretation.

You and I understand the noun "rock" differently if it appears in the sport's section of a newspaper, a music magazine, a geology textbook, and classic film noir crime drama about a jewelry heist. In order, the word would refer to a basketball or football, a type of music, a piece or mass of stone, and a gemstone. The word doesn't change, but its meaning varies dramatically. The meaning of a word is driven by context, and genre is context.

The serious Bible student must be aware of the importance of genre. Academic commentaries that engage the text as literature (as opposed to a devotional or homiletical approach) will pay close attention to genre. Make sure you have tools that alert you to genre in your Bible study arsenal.

CHAPTER 61

It's Okay When Bible Study Produces More than One Possible Interpretation

I hate movies that seem to intentionally end ambiguously. Love it or hate it, I want closure. I don't feel empowered by a director who lets me decide what their film meant. That just leaves me wondering why his or her mind was so clouded. Note to the director: the way to convince me you're brilliant isn't to show me you that you're incapable of precise thinking when it matters the most.

I've had some students that approach Bible study the same way. They simply can't tolerate the idea that there might truly be more than one interpretive option for a passage. The notion that alternatives exist disturbs them. The fact that those alternatives might be equally viable makes them break out in a cold sweat (or a rage, in my experience). I've never said it out loud, but I've thought it: "Please put your Strong's Concordance down and calmly walk away from that verse."

This sort of over-reaction telegraphs an emotional need for certainty. The thought that one's tradition, pastor, or parents might have been incorrect about something in the Bible produces a sense of vulnerability. That's unnecessary and, frankly, well beyond how God looks at the goals of Bible study.

Bible study shouldn't be fear-based. God does not expect

omniscience on the part of Bible students. He expects effort, humility, and a spirit of obedience to his will. Even if we don't (and we cannot) know with certainty what the Bible teaches in every passage, we can still apply what we're able to grasp (or think we've grasped) to our lives. Scripture is quite clear on fundamental virtues and vices, what pleases God and what offends him.

Another way to look at this has to do with the nature of Scripture. Resistance to uncertainty, however small, implies that there's nothing in Scripture that could realistically transcend our intellectual ability to comprehend with certainty. It's hard to consider that as anything but arrogance. As a scholar, I can tell you that the more I see in Scripture the more I realize I don't see. A Bible that's been all figured out would lose its intrigue—and importance. Thankfully, that isn't something we need to worry about.

CHAPTER 62

Pay Attention to How Biblical Writers Interpret Other Biblical Writers

B iblical writers didn't always produce original material. They used a variety of sources. This was especially true of New Testament writers. The reason is obvious, but sometimes overlooked: they had the Old Testament as a point of reference for what they had experienced and, therefore, what they wrote.

The New Testament writers cite the Old Testament hundreds of times. That sort of frequency demands attention. If you're going to be serious about Bible study, you cannot neglect observing what New Testament writers did with the Old Testament.

Unfortunately, failing at this simple strategy for understanding the Bible is something I've seen a multitude of times. The Bible students and pastors I've trained are largely ignorant of the importance of the Old Testament. The prevailing attitudes are that the Torah and the Historical books (Genesis through 2 Chronicles) only have value for character sketches. The poetic books are relegated to devotional reading. And the prophets become fodder for end times speculation, regardless of the fact that most prophecies you see were regarded as already fulfilled by the New Testament writers.

There are many reasons Bible students should pay attention to how New Testament writers cite the Old Testament.

For example, doing so would reveal that prophecy is not always fulfilled according to literal expectations. Matthew saw the emergency trip of Jesus to Egypt and back as a "fulfillment" of Hosea 11:1. But Hosea 11:1 isn't even a prophecy; it looks *backward* into Israel's history, not forward into the future. Matthew's point about Hosea is to strike an analogy between Israel and the Messiah, Jesus. The thought is an abstract one but theologically powerful.

Equally striking is how writers assign Old Testament verses that have God in view to Jesus. When John has Jesus telling the woman at the well that he would give her living water, it's no accident that he alludes to Jeremiah 17:13, which has God as the source of living water. The citation interchanges God and Jesus.

When the New Testament writers cite the Old Testament, they do so to make theological points. Observing them teaches us biblical theology. We would do well to see how biblical writers did their own Bible study.

CHAPTER 63

Tracing Concepts through the Bible Is More Profitable than Word Study

H ave you ever watched a movie where so much is happening in a scene that you invariably miss something important to the plot? That happens to me almost every time I watch a film adaptation of a Sherlock Holmes story. There are too many things to track simultaneously to really think like Sherlock. There's never just *one* thing that's important to notice in any given scene. The Bible is like that—repeatedly.

Developing skills in studying biblical words is important. But studying individual words often means only discerning one part of a set of ideas that's important to really understanding the meaning of a passage or biblical teaching. The theology of the Bible is often driven by clusters of concepts, each of which might involve one or more words. If you only do word study instead of looking for the clusters, your view of biblical theology will be fragmented.

A good illustration of this problem (and the solution) is the Old Testament concept of messiah. It may shock you, but of the nearly forty occurrences of the Hebrew term *mashiach*, less than a half dozen refer to a figure who would come well after the Old Testament period. This is because *mashiach* means "anointed" and is used throughout the Old Testament for Israelite kings and priests.

In other words, you can't get a theology of the Messiah from the word translated "messiah."

This fact notwithstanding, Jews living prior to the time of Jesus had a well-developed profile of what God's Messiah would be and do when he arrived. This was possible because the profile wasn't built on a word study of *mashiach*. Instead, it was built by clustering important concepts and observing how those concepts appeared together in various passages to form patterns of usage.

The concept of messiah really revolves around ideas associated with the restoration of Eden, faithfulness to God's commands, servanthood, kingship, and a priestly lineage outside Aaron and the tribe of Levi. Words associated with these themes tend to cluster in passages scattered through the Old Testament.

Careful Bible study therefore requires the student to detect and trace threads. Learn to observe terms that occur with other terms. Clustering patterns are often parts of a greater theological tapestry. Biblical writers didn't write unintentionally.

CHAPTER 64

The Bible Really Can Mean Exactly What It Says

Bible study can be something of an adventure. If you've been committed to a serious engagement with working through books of the Bible or topics that span its content, you know that what the Bible says can surprise you.

Sometimes, though, the Bible is uncomfortable, or painful, or even offensive. For example, our modern (and *human*) sensitivities won't allow us to feel at ease with prayers that ask God to violently kill an enemy (Ps. 109). It's repugnant to us that God would tell Joshua to annihilate all the occupants of a city (Josh. 6:15–21). We don't like the fact that the Law of Moses didn't allow women to inherit property (Num. 27), a situation rectified only by asking God's permission. It's disturbing to read that people who reject faith in Christ are condemned (John 3:18). I've met people who'd consider themselves Bible believers but who feel compelled to explain away ideas like the virgin birth (Matt. 1:21–25), giants in the Old Testament (Num. 13:32–33; Deut. 2–3), that God might tell someone to use deception (1 Sam. 16:1–13), and that God can prevent people from repenting (Isa. 6:8–13).

Our tendency in many of these instances is to look for interpretive strategies to make what the Bible says more palatable, to soften what it says or make its claims more reasonable to our minds.

It's true that we can indeed misunderstand the intent of a passage because the culture that produced it is thousands of years removed from us. But that cannot be an excuse for making a passage say what it didn't intend to say. That's dishonest. Sometimes the Bible really does mean exactly what it says, and we need to live with that.

Embracing the uncomfortable in the Bible is part of serious Bible study. We are studying God's Word as he prompted people to produce it, not as we'd like it to be. When its content troubles or offends us, we need to do our best to understand such passages in their own context, and from God's own perspective. Letting the Bible be what it is in its own time frame, culture, and setting won't always keep us from distress, but it will ultimately make sense on its own terms. Even the harshest, hardest passages to believe convey a theological message. Letting Scripture say what it says without changing it will ensure that we discern that message.

CHAPTER 65

Draw Both Positive and Negative Conclusions about What a Verse or Passage Teaches

Have you ever had a hard time putting exactly what you think into words? As a Bible scholar, I've experienced that many times. It's one thing to put the mental energy into studying Scripture—digging into Hebrew and Greek grammar, reading background material, evaluating translation choices, that sort of thing—and another thing altogether to be able to articulate what I'm finding. It can be frustrating.

The problem isn't writing or speaking; it's thinking with clarity. Here's some of the best advice I've ever received about clear thinking: to think with clarity, deliberately think about things both positively and negatively. A professor of mine once told us that the best way to come to a clear statement of what you believe is to express yourself in both affirmations (positive assertions) and denials (negative assertions).

The exercise of trying to say what you mean and following it by what you don't mean has a way of separating the mental chaff from the wheat. For example, let's take the statement in Romans 13:1 that says, "Let every person be subject to the governing authorities. For there is no authority except from God." You could say that you believe the verse teaches that every ruler on earth has been put there by God and should therefore be obeyed. But what exactly does that mean?

Do you mean to say there are no exceptions? How could you justify one? Is the verse an assertion of God's *activity* (God actually appoints every ruler) so that to disobey a ruler means rebelling against God's choice? Maybe it's just a statement of God's sovereignty without crediting God for every last tyrant on the planet. Or maybe Paul is just expressing a wish ("let everyone . . .") since he knows people can't change their circumstances under the Roman Empire. If your government allows you to replace a ruler, does this verse forbid that? Why would you want to replace someone God put in charge? What is it that you actually believe about this verse? What don't you believe?

A good way to sharpen your thinking, and your clarity in communicating to others, is to carefully consider the results of your Bible study in terms of what you think the text means and doesn't mean. It may take an hour or two—or even weeks—of thinking, but the result will be precision and clarity.

CHAPTER 66

Affirm the Obvious Without Extrapolating to the Unnecessary

Have you ever seen one of those shows about how aliens built the pyramids? Or maybe you remember *The DaVinci Code*—how a Christian sect in ancient Egypt believed Jesus was married, and so that must be a truth that all the other Christians in the world suppressed.

It's hard not to laugh, but a lot of people can't see the logical flaw in these examples. They may not believe such things, but they can't necessarily tell you what's wrong. They're classic examples of affirming an obvious truth and then extrapolating to unnecessary (and ridiculous) conclusions. In other words, the conclusion dramatically overstates the data. Yes, the pyramids are amazing. Archaeologists don't know with absolute certainty how they were built. But because they can't reproduce the feat doesn't mean aliens from space came here and did it. Yes, there were some people in the ancient church who believed Jesus was married, but that belief doesn't magically translate to reality.

I've talked about the need for logic and clear thinking in Bible study before. I'm not exaggerating when I say it's a critical tool for Bible study. I'm also serious when I say that its absence is apparent all over the place. The examples above are funny, but these hit closer to home:

- Paul praised the Mosaic law, so we should keep the Law, observe the Sabbath, and not worship on Sundays.
- Early Christians in Acts spoke in tongues, so every Christian needs to.
- Translations disagree, so we can't know what the Bible says.

These statements observe something obvious and then propose a far-flung conclusion that extends well beyond the observation. Christians are not commanded to observe the Law, though Paul had something nice to say about it. Christians in Acts spoke in tongues, but there is no command mandating it for everyone. Translations do disagree, but not everywhere, and most disagreements are not contradictory.

When we study Scripture, we will see things in the text. Every conclusion we draw should have a direct line back into the text. If it doesn't, our thinking goes beyond the text and is flawed.

PART 4

BIBLE STUDY TOOLS

CHAPTER 67

Learn about Strong's Numbers and Their Use

I was in high school when I finished reading the Bible for the first time. Once I finished, I intended to start over again, but I also wanted to start *studying* the Bible. I didn't really have an idea of how to do that, so I asked a friend whom I knew had studied the Bible for many years. He suggested a tool called *Strong's Exhaustive Concordance of the Bible*. That resource took me to a new level.

Strong's Concordance was the creation of Dr. James Strong (1822–1894), an American biblical scholar. Strong was a professor of biblical literature at Troy University in New York (1858–1861) and Drew Theological Seminary (1868–1894) in New Jersey. He first published his now famous concordance in 1890.

What exactly is a concordance? In simplest terms, it is an alphabetical listing of every word in an English translation along with a verse reference for that word. In the case of *Strong's Concordance*, the version he used was the King James Version. For example, you could use *Strong's Concordance* to look up the English word "love" and quickly see which verses have "love" in the Bible.

Strong's Concordance is more than a list, though. Strong, and a staff of over a hundred people who helped create the concordance, also created a numbering system for the Hebrew and Greek words behind the English translation. Using the word "love" again as our example, Strong's numbering system informs us that the Hebrew verb most often translated "love" was assigned the number 157. The Greek word most commonly translated "love" received the number 26. These numbers were used to create a dictionary in the back of the concordance. After finding the number, which appear sequentially, you will find a short definition that Strong and his assistants created for the Hebrew or Greek word corresponding to that number. Therefore, *Strong's Concordance* has an index of every word of the Bible in its original language.

Strong's numbering system has proved so popular and enduring that many biblical reference tools for helping English readers study Hebrew and Greek word meanings have adopted the system. *Strong's Concordance* is still in print, as are updated systems like the GK numbers. But in today's world of personal computers, print concordances have been superseded by digital versions and more powerful tools. Whether you use books or a computer, learning about concordance numbers can move you in a new direction for Bible study.

CHAPTER 68

Learn about Interlinear Bibles

Interlinear Bibles are one category of original language resources for Bible study that use concordance numbers. An interlinear simultaneously displays a line of an English translation and the corresponding line of the Hebrew or Greek biblical text.

A traditional interlinear shows the biblical Hebrew or Greek text on the top line and a literal English translation on the line below. Consequently, traditional interlinears follow the original language's word order, as that is the top line. Here is John 3:16 in a traditional interlinear. The numbers are GK numbers, which are—much like Strong's numbers—used in a dictionary that accompanies the interlinear.

¹⁶ Οὕτως γὰρ ἠγάπησεν ὁ θεὸς τὸν κόσμον ὥστε τὸν
οὕτως γάρ ἀγαπάω ὁ θεός ὁ κόσμος ὥστε ὁ
in this way₂ for₁ loved₄ — God₃ the world so that his₂ʷ
3779 1063 25 3588 2316 3588 2889 5620 3588

⌜υἱὸν τὸν μονογενῆ ἔδωκεν, ἵνα πᾶς ὁ πιστεύων
υἱός ὁ μονογενής δίδωμι ἵνα πᾶς ὁ πιστεύω
Son₄ — one and only₃ he gave₁ in order that everyone — who believes
5207 3588 3439 1325 2443 3956 3588 4100

εἰς αὐτὸν μὴ ἀπόληται ἀλλὰ ἔχῃ ζωὴν αἰώνιον.
εἰς αὐτός μή ἀπόλλυμι ἀλλά ἔχω ζωή αἰώνιος
in him [will] not perish but will have life₂ eternal₁
1519 846 3361 622 235 2192 2222 166

Interlinears can be found in book form as well as in computer software. In a digital environment, interlinears are a powerful tool for original language research. English readers can find every occurrence of a Hebrew or Greek word in the Bible in less than one second. From that point, hyperlinks to specialized dictionaries for biblical Hebrew and Greek are one click away.

The disadvantage to a traditional interlinear Bible is that you can't simply read the English in order. We'll talk about an interlinear that solves that problem in the next chapter: the *reverse* interlinear.

CHAPTER 69

Learn about Reverse Interlinears and Their Use

In the previous chapter, I introduced interlinear Bibles—specifically, those in a traditional interlinear format. An even more powerful tool is the reverse interlinear.

Like traditional interlinears, a reverse interlinear displays lines of English and the original biblical language. The traditional interlinear format has the Hebrew or Greek line on top, which means the English word order is disrupted. *Unlike* traditional interlinears, a reverse interlinear puts the English line on the top. Here is John 3:16 in a reverse interlinear display.

16 " For	h	God	so	loved	i the	world	,9 i	that	he
γὰρ$_2$	ὁ$_4$	θεὸς$_5$	οὕτως$_1$	ἠγάπησεν$_3$	τὸν$_6$	κόσμον$_7$		ὥστε$_8$	→
γάρ	ὁ	θεός	οὕτως	ἀγαπάω	ὁ	κόσμος		ὥστε	
1063	3588	2316	3779	25	3588	2889		5620	

gave	his	only	Son	,	that	whoever	believes	in
ἔδωκεν$_{13}$	τὸν$_9$	τὸν$_{11}$ μονογενῆ$_{12}$	υἱὸν$_{10}$		ἵνα$_{14}$	πᾶς$_{15}$ ὁ$_{16}$	πιστεύων$_{17}$	εἰς$_{18}$
δίδωμι	ὁ	ὁ μονογενής	υἱός		ἵνα	πᾶς ὁ	πιστεύω	εἰς
1325	3588	3588 3439	5207		2443	3956 3588	4100	1519

him	should	not	k	perish	but	have	eternal	life	.
αὐτὸν$_{19}$	►21	μὴ$_{20}$		ἀπόληται$_{21}$	ἀλλ'$_{22}$	ἔχη$_{23}$	αἰώνιον$_{25}$	ζωὴν$_{24}$	
αὐτός		μή		ἀπόλλυμι	ἀλλά	ἔχω	αἰώνιος	ζωή	
846		3361		622	235	2192	166	2222	

An obvious advantage to the reverse interlinear format is its readability. It has the correct English word order. And concordance numbers are included. But the advantages go beyond the aesthetic. Reverse interlinears in Bible software allow Bible students to link to many tools for Hebrew and Greek word research that don't use concordance numbers. The reason is that the creation of a reverse interlinear involves directly linking each word of the translation to the Hebrew or Greek word from which it derives.

CHAPTER 70

Use More than One Translation in Bible Study

The wording of my advice for the day is deliberate. I could have said, "Use more than one translation *for* Bible study," but I didn't. I'm recommending that you use more than one translation *in* Bible study. There's an important difference.

The first option might lead you to think that I'm advising you to switch Bible versions from time to time when you study Scripture. That isn't the case. Rather, I'm suggesting that you have several translations at hand while you're studying. That's why I chose to word my advice as I did.

Having several English Bible versions open is very useful for detecting something in a verse or passage that might deserve serious attention in your study. Let's look at a couple examples. The first one is Genesis 49:10.

NASB (1995)	ESV
The scepter shall not depart from Judah, Nor the ruler's staff from between his feet, *Until Shiloh comes*, And to him *shall be* the obedience of the peoples.	The scepter shall not depart from Judah, nor the ruler's staff from between his feet, *until tribute comes to him*; and to him shall be the obedience of the peoples.

The two translations are quite different in the boldfaced portion. If you were using more than one translation, you'd notice that easily. If you were just switching translations for a while, you'd never see that. A clear difference like this is a signal that there's something going on in the original biblical text that matters for interpretation. Let's look at Romans 8:1 this time.

ESV	NKJV
There is therefore now no condemnation for those who are in Christ Jesus.	There is therefore now no condemnation to those who are in Christ Jesus, *who do not walk according to the flesh, but according to the Spirit.*

Again, there's a dramatic difference. The NKJV is twice as long. And the difference matters. The NKJV seems to suggest that one reason we're not condemned is that we're living (walking) in the Spirit as we should. Are works part of the reason we are not under condemnation? How good must we be? We need to study what's going on here to find out. And now you know because you compared translations.

CHAPTER 71

Read a Book—or Take a Course— on Biblical Hermeneutics

Hermeneutics is the science and art of interpretation. It should be distinguished from Bible study methods. Hermeneutics uses involved processes in interpretation, but it also includes historical and theoretical issues and problems.

When it comes to historical and theoretical issues, a hermeneutics book or course will typically discuss things like the following:

- *The history of biblical interpretation.* The Bible has not always been interpreted with the methods we use today. For example, the ancient Jewish community and the early church fathers employed techniques that we would consider strange or even inadvisable today. The same can be said for other periods of church history.

- *Historical and cultural analysis.* A hermeneutics course would introduce students to tools for learning about the civilizations and worldviews that surrounded the ancient Israelites. These resources include primary sources—literature produced by ancient Egyptians or Romans, for example. Serious Bible students need to know where to find primary sources and which literary works contribute to understanding what's written in the Bible.

- *Applying the Bible across modern cultures.* This area deals with theoretical and practical approaches for communicating the Bible to the world's cultures. Even in our own day we know that cultural differences interfere with accurate communication. This is even more true in regard to a book as ancient as the Bible.

In terms of methods of analyzing the biblical text, a hermeneutics book or course will introduce students to a range of procedures, including:

- *Proper methods of word study.* The student needs to consider issues like word usage in context and how synonyms relate to each other.
- *Literary genre.* Genre refers to a type of literature, and genre influences meaning (you wouldn't interpret the word "court" the same way in a legal document, a sports column, and a building permit).
- *Greek and Hebrew grammar.* Students need to understand grammatical terms that commentaries use when they interact with the original text. For instance, it matters what a Greek "aorist tense" is and how it affects meaning.

There's a lot to consider when you're studying Scripture, and one of the major goals is proper interpretation. For that, exposure to a hermeneutics textbook or course is indispensable.

CHAPTER 72
Discover Bible Commentaries

I've been addicted to Bible study since becoming a Christian in high school. And *addicted* is the right word. Once I had read through the Bible as a sophomore, I moved on to Strong's numbers and a concordance. After a year of that, I wanted something else. One happy, glorious morning (okay, I'm embellishing a little) I discovered commentaries. I wasn't quite in Bible "nerdvana," but I could see it over the horizon. Honestly, what public high school senior takes commentaries to school to read in study hall? Been there, done that.

In case you still haven't discovered commentaries, I should explain what they are. For those of you who already know (and for those who will know after hitting the bottom of this page), I'll be spending some time in another chapter on the different types of commentaries. They're certainly not all created equal.

A commentary is a book about the Bible, but not in the sense that the author is strictly talking about the Bible's history, backgrounds, sections, characters, or theology. A commentary guides the reader through the Bible, either section by section or verse by verse. It's as though you have your own private scholar watching over your shoulder as you read the Bible, and that scholar takes time to comment (hence "commentary") on what you're reading. Commentaries partner you with an experienced student of Scripture to help you study.

Commentaries differ widely in the level of detail contained in comments about what the Bible says. But one thing they have in common is the goal to take the user beyond merely reading their translation of the Bible. A commentary is naturally geared to help you pause and reflect on the material. That might mean discussing the possible meanings of a particular word, alerting you to how some element of ancient culture explains a particular phrase, or making a historical observation that situates the content of the passage in a particular time period or civilization.

Commentaries also seek to highlight how a passage or book provides practical insights for wise living and deepening your relationship with God. After all, the Bible is no mere collection of facts. It's about a relationship with God through Christ. Commentaries don't just inform. They can rebuke and encourage as well.

CHAPTER 73

Buy Bible Software—Then Use It

Full disclosure: I work for a Bible software company, Logos Bible Software. Here's another disclosure: I used Bible software before I began to work for Logos. I'd recommend that you buy (and use) Bible software no matter what my circumstances were. Unless you'd rather have a rotary phone, like to wash dishes and clothes by hand, or yearn for the days of the Ford Model T, *you want Bible software*. I realize there might be some people out there in the world that have enough time to experience the thrill of spending weeks or months on a Bible study task that my software can do in less than a second, but I'm not that guy. We still have monks and monasteries, but the monastic age is history.

There's nothing like having Bible software when it comes to Bible study. It isn't an issue of laziness or wanting to do Bible study as fast as possible to move on to the rest of your day. No way. Bible study still takes discipline; it isn't a ritual act. That really isn't what lightning speed for processing searches in the Bible is about. The speed allows you to get *more* done, not pave the way to do less. This is what technology is all about: how to do something with greater accuracy, efficiency, and frequency. Bible software is a boon in all those respects.

In the old days (forty years ago, not the days of the apostles), scholars had a few reference works that would enable them to do tasks like look up all the occurrences of a word in the Bible. But they would have to manually navigate to each passage to make sure that the hand work responsible for that reference work was accurate. And even then, the tools to search for anything beyond a single word, or for words in books besides the Bible, just didn't exist.

All of that is a reality today. This is particularly true because of Bible software companies' massive biblical studies libraries. You can find discussions of anything you're looking for in thousands of books all at the same time, even in books that have no indexes of their own. Bible software also enables Bible students who don't read Hebrew and Greek to search in those languages. There's literally nothing like it on the planet.

CHAPTER 74

Acquire a Clear, Succinct Theological Dictionary

When you're engaged in serious Bible study, you will invariably end up running into theology. The Bible is not simply putting forth names, places, and events in artful storytelling. It's teaching truths to believe—truths about God, about us, and about God's solution for the human condition and human destiny. That's theology, the study of God and what He's about. So don't panic if you end up thinking about doctrine. That's supposed to happen.

I say it that way since lots of Christians I know recoil at theology, either because they think it's impractical and boring, or it scares them. Having had a lot of experience in the formal study (and teaching) of theology, that's understandable. Theologians use a lot of terms that are long and unfamiliar. But despite the confusing nature of many such terms, they're important to know, since you won't be able to avoid them in academic reading in theology. And you need to look up words in books you don't know. To avoid that is to remain ignorant, which isn't a virtue in Bible study (or anything else).

There are two convenient solutions to this problem. One is to have some good theology books with indexes. At the very least you can see if the index has that word that stopped you cold. You might get a nice definition on one of the pages to which the index directs you. Using Bible software, of course, makes this basically effortless.

The problem with this solution is that your theology books may not have the term you're looking for in the index (presuming there is one). And even then, you may not get a short, clear definition. Enter the second solution: get a succinct theological dictionary. I'm not talking about a reference work that has long articles on topics. I'm talking about a dictionary that defines terms in a couple of sentences.

There are a couple of options that fit this description. My favorite, and the one I think is the best, is Millard Erickson's *Concise Dictionary of Christian Theology*. The book is exactly what the title claims. It has hundreds of theological terms defined in short, understandable sentences. With this tool in hand, you never need fear reading a theology book. It should be part of every Bible student's arsenal.

CHAPTER 75

Use the Net Bible

I'm the kind of person who likes to use things until they can no longer be fixed. I don't like to upgrade until whatever I'm using passes the point of being inconvenient but workable to being totally useless, even dangerous. Admit it: we all have something that's "good enough" for what we need to do. And if we're just as honest, we also have to admit that when we do upgrade we wonder why we waited so long.

That's how it will be with the NET Bible.

What's the NET Bible? Close your eyes and think about the study Bible you're using. Can you see the tiny footnotes scattered through your translation here and there? They direct your attention to a few words at the bottom of the page, maybe a suggestion for another translation or something about a manuscript. There aren't that many, but they're useful. Got that fixed in your mind? Now give your study Bible a performance-enhancing drug, maybe a growth hormone. The NET Bible is what all other study Bibles want to be when they grow up.

I'm not kidding. The NET Bible is a freely available translation created by dozens of scholars experienced in Bible translation. It has over 60,000 notes, most of which explain specifically why the translators did what they did or how a different manuscript reading might affect translation. The preface to the NET Bible explains why it's distinctive:

The translators' notes make the original languages far more accessible, allowing you to look over the translator's shoulder at the very process of translation. This level of documentation is a first for a Bible translation, making transparent the textual basis and the rationale for key renderings (including major interpretive options and alternative translations).

There's no other tool that comes close to it for English readers who don't know Greek and Hebrew. If you are growing in your Bible study skills, at some point you need to breach the English translation. The NET Bible has an unparalleled focus on the biblical text and the decisions the English translators made.

CHAPTER 76

All Commentaries Are Not Created Equal

Of the many tools for Bible study available today, commentaries are among the most familiar. A commentary might be a tool you associate with your pastor, but they should be used by every serious Bible student. But all commentaries are not the same.

There are basically three different kinds of commentaries: devotional, expositional, and scholarly. They have widely different aims. Here is a sampling of their attributes.

Devotional:
- English-only focus
- Surface-level observations that often repeat the English translation
- Usually not verse-by-verse
- Comments aimed at practical application
- Gives the reader an interpretation
- No analysis of other views
- Moderate cross-referencing
- May include advice for preaching or teaching

Expositional:

- Focus on the English text, but comments on the original languages
- Usually verse-by-verse
- Some attempt to take the reader through interpretive options
- Offers nontechnical background material
- Occasional discussion of variant manuscript readings
- Occasional discussion of literary features (e.g., parallelism, genre)

Scholarly:

- The writer includes his or her own translation
- Verse-by-verse, word-by-word
- Detailed discussion of original languages, parallel ancient literature, literary features, and manuscript variations
- Concerted effort at informing the reader of all interpretive options

The more you develop skills in Bible study, including either learning some Hebrew and Greek or mastering original language tools, you'll be able to make use of all different types of commentaries.

CHAPTER 77

Learn How to Do Word Studies

S ome of my earlier suggestions for Bible study included learning about the numbering system in concordances and reverse
interlinears. Both provide assistance for doing word studies. You
need to know how to properly study biblical words in their original
languages. Word studies are an important strategy for penetrating
your English translation to gain insights for interpretation. Today
I want to introduce the concept.

Learning how to study the Hebrew and Greek words behind
your English translation is important for some simple reasons. One
is that a wide range of English words in your translation might be
translating the same original language word. That is, there is no
one-for-one correspondence between the English word you read
and an original language word. Many English Bible readers don't
realize this. When they do, it prompts some obvious questions: Why
don't translators use the same English word each time the original
language word occurs? Shouldn't they do that to be consistent in
translation?

Another reason is the reverse of the above: a wide range of
original language words might all get the same English word
in a translation. Like English, Hebrew and Greek words have
synonyms—words whose meanings are closely related (e.g., canine,
dog, hound, pooch). There's definite overlap with those terms, but
there is also nuanced meaning. So it is with Hebrew and Greek.

But you'll never discover Hebrew and Greek synonyms if you can't do word studies. Synonyms also prompt questions: Why would the biblical writer choose one word over another? Was he trying to communicate something by the choice?

Doing word study requires (a) detecting the original language word behind the English word, (b) finding all occurrences of that word, (c) asking good interpretive questions about how that word is used by biblical writers, and (d) having access to tools that analyze and discuss the meaning of original language words according to their usage in the Bible.

In the next few chapters, I'll discuss some of the requirements for word study. I'll also talk about how not to study words—logical fallacies in word study that lead to false conclusions and flawed interpretation. For now, realize that you're at the mercy of translators unless you can get beyond your translation. Word study is a key to doing that.

CHAPTER 78

When Studying Biblical Words, Pay Attention to Word Distribution

Word study involves more than just looking up original language words in a word study dictionary (a lexicon). The usage of a word in context is the most important consideration. However, there are times when a word's distribution within either a book or in the writings of a single author ought to influence the way we think about word meaning.

One of the best examples of this consideration is the Greek noun translated "unmarried" (*agamos*). This word occurs four times in the New Testament—all in the same chapter and, therefore, all by the same author. The fact that only Paul uses this term four times in 1 Corinthians 7 means that we must allow what Paul writes (and, in this case, what he doesn't) to inform our understanding of the word's meaning. Put negatively, it matters not how some author in some other Greek text from some other period says. We have to figure out what *Paul* was thinking when he used the word.

On the surface, "unmarried" seems easy to define. It's "the state of being spouseless." Fair enough, but there are a number of different circumstances that would put someone in that category. Here are the circumstances that would mean you have no spouse:

- Never been married
- Your spouse has died
- Divorced
- Your spouse has deserted you

The last circumstance is less familiar to us than people (usually women) in the ancient world. Scholars agree that Paul's language in 1 Corinthians 7 includes all four circumstances. They disagree, however, on whether Paul would have forbidden remarriage to those divorced. The answer to that question depends on whether it seems reasonable (or not) to presume that Paul included divorce as a circumstance for being spouseless in verses 27–28. Is Paul talking *only* about first-time marriage in those verses, or is anyone "loosed" from a spouse allowed to remarry? Answering that question is the interpretive task in 1 Corinthians 7. There is nowhere else to look for what this term might include or exclude in any given verse, since it occurs only here.

CHAPTER 79

Bible Software Should Be a Tool for Bible Study, Not a Crutch

You know by now how I feel about Bible software. It's an essential tool for Bible study. If you can navigate Facebook or check email, you can use Bible software. It's time to rush boldly into the twenty-first century.

Think about it. We use technology for almost everything. And if you're an adult, a lot of that technology is recent. That means there was a time you didn't have it and used something else. That in turn means you *were* able to learn it and take advantage of the benefits. If you can take pictures of yourself doing embarrassing, pointless things and upload them for millions of people you don't know to see, then you can learn how to use Bible software.

The only real trick to Bible software is discovering what you can do with it. That works two ways. Bible software can replicate what you currently do with amazing speed and visual clarity. In other words, it can help you with all the strategies you enjoy now. But Bible software can also help you get to information in ways you've never imagined. Old dogs *can* learn new tricks.

Logos Bible Software is my tool of choice. Not only does it help me with original language research, but it's a library. I've already talked about original language tools and software. I want to focus on the library here.

We know what libraries and books are. But having a digital library in a software platform is like also having a research assistant. With one click you can run through thousands of volumes for a topic. Yesterday's Bible study meant flipping a book open to see if it had an index that included the topic word you're looking for. But what if the book doesn't have an index? In a software environment, that isn't an issue. Your research assistant has all your books memorized. The result is discovering help you didn't know was available.

The danger with having supercharged tools is that they become a crutch. That can happen. People will encounter the temptation to just copy and paste what they find into their Bible study notes without analyzing the information. You pile on information without assessing the content. It's like buying books that you never read. Remember: there is no substitute for thinking when it comes to Bible study—not even software.

CHAPTER 80

Become Familiar with Bible Reference Works

Recommending that a Bible student become familiar with Bible reference works is like suggesting to a carpenter that he get familiar with a hammer, saw, and drill. Reference works are crucial tools for any serious Bible study. In this chapter, I'd like to acquaint you with the different types of reference works for Bible study.

There are several things to look for in any given reference work.

First, you want it to be the product of specialists. Most major academic publishers keep a sharp eye on this sort of thing because their reference works won't sell to libraries, the biggest buyer of reference material, without such expertise. That means you can avoid a substandard work by making sure the publisher has a long track record of producing reference material.

Second, you want it to be up-to-date. The typical life cycle of a reference work in biblical studies is twenty years. Time marches on. In the span of a few decades, archaeologists, historians, linguists, and biblical studies scholars discover new things and new ways of analyzing the Bible. For instance, a biblical reference work produced in the year before the Dead Sea Scrolls were discovered became out-of-date long before the twenty-year cycle!

More specifically, there are different types of reference works. Most people hear the phrase "reference work" and think of encyclopedias. That's certainly a major category. Encyclopedias relevant for biblical studies might be devoted to the Bible itself, but encyclopedias of the ancient Near East or ancient Greece and Rome are also quite important for serious Bible study.

Not all reference works are encyclopedias. Bible dictionaries are similar but not quite the same thing. There are exceptions, but Bible dictionaries are usually shorter and therefore not as exhaustive. They are most often one-volume works, while encyclopedias tend to be multivolume sets.

Bible atlases are reference works. Every Bible student should have a good Bible atlas, which is not only filled with maps but also some discussion about places and incidents marked on the maps.

Related to reference works specifically about the Bible are theological reference works. There are many specialized dictionaries aimed at theological topics.

There are other types of reference, but these are the major categories.

Printed in the USA
CPSIA information can be obtained
at www.ICGtesting.com
LVHW032053290723
753738LV00007B/71